T0288644

Praise for *The Great Dechurching*

Every church leader—either lay leader or ordained—needs to read this book to understand who is leaving churches, why they are leaving, and what it will take to bring them back. *The Great Dechurching* overflows with practical wisdom about the sobering reality of dechurching. While there is top level assessment of the numbers, the heart of the book is about people we all know and love. I am giving copies of this book to the clergy in the diocese where I serve, and I will assign it for the seminary courses I teach.

—**Justin S. Holcomb,** bishop of the Episcopal Diocese
of Central Florida, seminary professor, and author

If you know someone who used to go to church and now doesn't, this book is for you. Jim Davis and Michael Graham have written a timely, necessary, and extremely beneficial resource that will compel and prepare those of us in the church to reach out to those who have left. *The Great Dechurching* is full of robust research that offers real hope and true help. This might be one of the most significant books you will read. May God use it to call many back to his beloved bride, the church.

—**Courtney Doctor,** director of women's initiatives at
The Gospel Coalition, Bible teacher, and author of *From
Garden to Glory, In View of God's Mercies,* and others

We all know that an annual physical is important; most of us also see it as more of an inconvenience than anything else. But talk to one close friend or family member who discovers a life-threatening health issue that could have been prevented had they not neglected their physical for years, and suddenly the annual checkup seems like less of a hassle. After ignoring obvious symptoms for decades, the church needs lab work to assess her health. In *The Great Dechurching,* Jim Davis and Michael Graham with researcher Ryan Burge do just that, and their diagnosis is generally not encouraging. But the book does far more than offer an empirical diagnosis. They offer a plan of care for the church that can lead to renewed life in our churches, the return of many dechurched, and a greater gospel impact in our world.

—**Ed Stetzer, PhD,** professor and dean, Talbot School of Theology

This is one of those books I wish did not have to be written—but it did—on a topic I wish we didn't have to think about—but we do. I am so glad Jim Davis, Michael Graham, and Ryan Burge have teamed up to do it. We need responsible voices analyzing what is happening, and that makes me especially grateful for the way these authors approach the subject of dechurching.

This book is a clarion call, but it is not without hope or counsel. Instead of the mere pragmatism that often characterizes projects like this, the authors offer theological, confessional, and catechetical recommendations with ecclesiological convictions. The reader will still have to do the hard work of application to his or her own situation, but the reflection and action this book will spark could be significant. God is always up to something in moments like this, and we want to respond in wisdom and faithfulness to be instruments for his good purposes.

—**Ligon Duncan,** chancellor and CEO, Reformed Theological Seminary

Many Christian leaders and commentators have commented on trends in American church life. All of them will find something in *The Great Dechurching* that surprises them. But the appeal of this book isn't just bound up in the data it shares, as valuable as that is. Graham and Davis offer much in the way of shrewd analysis of the data and sober reflection on what it means for the life of the church in America. That analysis and reflection both elevate the book and offer to followers of Jesus a vision for how the next chapter of the Christian movement in America can be better than the one now coming to a close.

—**Jake Meador,** editor-in-chief, *Mere Orthodoxy*

Few things break my heart like watching friends leave the church behind. *The Great Dechurching* starts with bad news: I'm not alone. America is undergoing the largest, fastest religious shift in its history. Forty million people have left the church. But there's still hope. Many dechurched Americans are open to coming back. Using insights drawn from Jim Davis and Michael Graham's writing, we've welcomed hundreds of dechurched people into our local church community, where they can encounter Jesus and construct life-changing relationships.

—**Patrick Miller,** pastor, author, and cohost of *Truth over Tribe*

The Great Dechurching

The Great De church ing

Who's Leaving, Why Are They Going, and What Will It Take to Bring Them Back?

Jim Davis and Michael Graham

with Ryan P. Burge

Foreword by Collin Hansen

ZONDERVAN
REFLECTIVE

ZONDERVAN REFLECTIVE

The Great Dechurching
Copyright © 2023 by James Davis and Michael S. Graham

Published in Grand Rapids, Michigan, by Zondervan. Zondervan is a registered trademark
of The Zondervan Corporation, L.L.C., a wholly owned subsidiary of HarperCollins
Christian Publishing, Inc.
Requests for information should be addressed to customercare@harpercollins.com.

Zondervan titles may be purchased in bulk for educational, business, fundraising, or sales
promotional use. For information, please email SpecialMarkets@Zondervan.com.

ISBN 978-0-310-14588-2 (audio)

Library of Congress Cataloging-in-Publication Data

Names: Davis, Jim (Pastor), author. | Graham, Michael S., author. | Burge, Ryan P. author.
Title: The great dechurching : who's leaving, why are they going, and what will it take to
    bring them back? / Jim Davis, Michael S. Graham, Ryan Burge.
Description: Grand Rapids : Zondervan, 2023.
Identifiers: LCCN 2023009932 (print) | LCCN 2023009933 (ebook) | ISBN 9780310147435
    (hardcover) | ISBN 9780310145875 (ebook)
Subjects: LCSH: Ex-church members. | Church work with ex-church members. | Church
    attendance—United States. | Non-church-affiliated people United States. | BISAC:
    RELIGION / Christian Church / General | RELIGION / Christian Living / Social Issues
Classification: LCC BV4523 .D38 2023 (print) | LCC BV4523 (ebook) | DDC 262—dc23/
    eng/20230425
LC record available at https://lccn.loc.gov/2023009932
LC ebook record available at https://lccn.loc.gov/2023009933

Cover design and photography: Micah Kandros Design
Interior design: Sara Colley

Printed in the United States of America

24 25 26 27 28 LBC 10 9 8 7 6

To our church family at Orlando Grace Church

Contents

Part 1: Meet the Dechurched

Part 2: Profiles of the Dechurched

Part 3: Engaging the Dechurched

Part 4: Lessons for the Church

Table of Figures

Foreword

WE'RE LIVING AMID THE LARGEST AND FASTEST TRANSFORMATION OF religion in American history, what Jim Davis and Michael Graham describe as the "Great Dechurching." Aided by Ryan Burge, this book deploys the best cutting-edge research on some forty million Americans who have left the church in the last twenty-five years. You'll find in this book the most comprehensive, detailed reasons that our friends, family, and neighbors have left the church.

But Davis and Graham don't leave church leaders in despair. They show us the reasons these millions might return to the church. They write with pastoral perspective on the kinds of churches that can thrive in our secular age. Best of all, they ground their counsel in biblical and theological reflection that has sustained God's people for thousands of years.

We have no reason to fear even if the church across the West continues to lose political and cultural power. After all, consider the context of the Bible itself. In Daniel 1:12–13, the titular brave young man knows he's playing with house money, even though he's been torn away from his home and carried away in exile. Daniel acts like he knows the final score of the game before it's even played—you try your diet, and we'll try ours. His tone is less defiant than confident. Why isn't he phased? Because his heart belongs to God, no matter where he lives. He's not anxious. Babylon is only his temporary home. He'll serve there with distinction. But his heart belongs with

God, who is the Beginning and the End, the Alpha and the Omega, the Lord of Babylon and Jerusalem.

By contrast, many American Christians today suffer from anxiety because they feel like they've lost their home. They may not have been taken away from their houses and land and churches. But they don't feel like their nation or state or city feels like home any longer.

When we're anxious and afraid, we get angry. And no one wants an angry neighbor.

Daniel, however, was a great neighbor. In Daniel 1:17 we see how he blesses Babylon and King Nebuchadnezzar.

Daniel knew where he lived: Babylon. Where do we live? My home city, Birmingham, is Babylon. My home state, Alabama, is Babylon. The United States of America is Babylon.

Three times in the New Testament we see that exile is our status as believers in Christ until Jesus returns or calls us home. One of these passages is Hebrews 11:13–16, which urges Christians to follow the example of faith shown by the saints of the Old Testament:

> These all died in faith, not having received the things promised, but having seen them and greeted them from afar, and having acknowledged that they were strangers and exiles on the earth. For people who speak thus make it clear that they are seeking a homeland. If they had been thinking of that land from which they had gone out, they would have had opportunity to return. But as it is, they desire a better country, that is, a heavenly one. Therefore God is not ashamed to be called their God, for he has prepared for them a city. (ESV)

Daniel belongs in this hall of faith, these heroes of the Old Testament who anticipated the Savior to come. As God's Son, Jesus Christ wasn't dragged kicking and screaming from his home at the Father's right hand. He came to Babylon willingly! To rescue us. He endured exile so that all who repent of their sins and believe in him could go home.

We might live in Babylon right now, but thanks to Christ, one day we'll live in New Jerusalem. We're in exile now. But soon we'll be home.

Until then, *The Great Dechurching* will help you live by faith in Babylon.

Collin Hansen
Executive Director
The Keller Center for Cultural Apologetics

Introduction

THE SPIRITUAL LANDSCAPE OF OUR CITY, ORLANDO, FLORIDA, HAS changed more than most could have imagined thirty years ago. In the 1990s and early 2000s, Orlando looked like it would be the new Christian Mecca. First Presbyterian Church was the second-largest mainline church in the nation. First Baptist Church was booming, and their pastor was president of the Southern Baptist Convention. Northland Church, pastored by Joel Hunter, grew to more than twenty thousand people. He has served as a spiritual adviser to the president of the United States and now serves on the board of the National Association of Evangelicals.[1] His son Isaac planted a church downtown that drew thousands of millennials and even some NBA players, including Dwight Howard. Reformed Theological Seminary expanded to Orlando, and soon after, the largest parachurch missions agency in the world, Campus Crusade for Christ, relocated its headquarters here. R. C. Sproul and Ligonier, Wycliffe, Pioneers, and about a dozen other Christian ministries followed suit. Every aspect of the theological spectrum seemed to be booming in Orlando as Benny Hinn and Paula White also pastored churches here. Now Orlando has the same percentage

---

1. Kate Shellnutt, "Joel Hunter Is Done Pastoring His Orlando Megachurch," *Christianity Today*, August 2, 2017, https://www.christianitytoday.com/news/2017/august/joel-hunter -stepping-down-northland-senior-pastor-orlando.html.

of evangelicals as New York City and Seattle[2] as 42 percent[3] (roughly 2 million people) of our metropolitan area have stopped attending church. We call them the *dechurched*.

What has happened here is happening all over the country. The national aspect of this phenomenon hit me when I (Jim) was giving a brief talk at a donor event for a global ministry with attenders from all over the country. I spoke for about ten minutes about dechurching and was followed by a nationally known pastor who gave a great, more general gospel-centered keynote message.

After the evening session was finished, people lined up to speak with me, ask me questions, and give me business cards, offering to help in any way with our work. In a somewhat surreal moment, I looked over to see the other speaker getting coffee by himself. I was confused at first, but the logic soon settled in. He was the better speaker with the bigger platform, but when it came to dechurching, I was talking about this audience's friends, children, and grand-children. They had seen the people they love most depart from the institution they need the most: the church. The dechurched aren't just numbers on a spreadsheet; they are people we know and love.

What began as a desire to equip our local church through a podcast called *As in Heaven*, became a research project that eventually developed into this book. Our desire to effectively reach the dechurched in Orlando and to help prevent more dechurching unexpectedly took on a national scope. We had anecdotal observations and experiences with the dechurched, but those could get us only so far. There wasn't much data available, and what was out there was older and wasn't going through academic review boards. We could find nothing recent that comprehensively explained why people are leaving, where they are going, and what we can do to bring them back.

---

2. Barna Report Orlando, Daytona Beach, Melbourne 2017–2018 Report.
3. 2018 Barna Report on Metro Orlando.

It isn't hard to see the spiritual landscape changing fast, but we desired something more than our street-level view. We needed reliable, science-driven data, and thanks to the generosity of like-minded people, we were able to raise significant funds to make this data possible. We engaged social scientists Dr. Ryan Burge and Dr. Paul Djupe to do an academic-review-board-approved, nationwide, quantitative study to answer our questions about the dechurching phenomenon.

Dr. Ryan Burge is a political scientist at Eastern Illinois University, where he is also the graduate coordinator. His work focuses on the interaction of religion and political behavior, especially in the American context. In addition, he is the research director for Faith Counts, a nonprofit, nondenominational organization that promotes the social value of faith. He is the author of *The Nones: Where They Came From, Who They Are, and Where They Are Going* and *20 Myths about Religion and Politics in America*.

Dr. Paul Djupe is a political scientist at Denison University, directing the Data for Political Research minor and specializing in religion and politics, social networks, gender and politics, and political behavior. He is an affiliated scholar with Public Religion Research Institute and the editor of the Religious Engagement in Democratic Politics series with Temple University Press. He has authored, coauthored, or edited eight books that focus on religion and politics.

When the results of our study came in, not only were our basic hunches confirmed, but the results were more shocking than we expected. The size, pace, and scope of dechurching in America is at such historic levels that there is no better phrase to describe this phenomenon than the Great Dechurching.

The Three Phases

The research conducted by Burge and Djupe was collected in three phases. In each stage, the research team contracted with research industry standard Qualtrics[4] to find survey respondents and to ensure the academic reliability of each participant. For each of the three surveys, the instrument was approved by the Institutional Review Board (IRB) at Denison University. The goal of the IRB process is to ensure that no harm will be done to those who participate in the research, and that their privacy and anonymity will be ensured by the research team. In all three cases, IRB approved the survey without issue.

Phase 1: How Big Is the Problem?

For the purposes of our study, we defined a dechurched person as someone who used to go to church at least once per month but now goes less than once a year. The first phase of the study was simple. We sought to prove or disprove this thesis: *We are currently in the middle of the largest and fastest religious shift in the history of our country.* This phase included a population size of 1,043 American adults.

The data we collected overwhelmingly supported our thesis. Before now, the largest religious shift in church attendance in the US occurred during the twenty-five-year period after the Civil War.[5] From 1870 to 1895, church attendance more than doubled as people resumed their postwar lives.[6] That religious shift pales in comparison to what we are seeing today, only instead of going back to church, people today are leaving church. About 15 percent of American adults living today (around 40 million people) have effectively stopped going to church, and most of this dechurching has happened in the past twenty-five years.

Something important to note is that only phase 1 of this project

---

4. Qualtrics has been used in the publication of hundreds of papers in peer-reviewed outlets across the social sciences, and data collected in this manner is seen by scholars as being of very high quality.

5. Roger Finke and Rodney Stark, *The Churching of America, 1776–2005* (New Brunswick, NJ: Rutgers University Press, 2005), 23, fig. 1.2.

6. Finke and Stark, 23, fig. 1.2.

was focused on collecting a general sample equivalent of the American population. In phases 2 and 3, Qualtrics was given subsample quotas to meet in terms of dechurched Americans and dechurched evangelicals. This means that only the data collected in phase 1 can be used to estimate the rate of dechurching in the United States.

Phase 2: Who Is Leaving and Why?

The aim of phase 2 of the study was to compare differences and similarities between churched and dechurched people from all religious traditions. It included a population size of 4,099 dechurched American adults. In phases 2 and 3, the main goal of the data collection was to produce a data set meaningfully large enough for a machine-learning algorithm to create profiles of different types of dechurched persons. Hence, all those who took part in these later surveys were themselves dechurched.

This means that in spite of the large sample size, when we write that a certain percentage of the dechurched people in our sample fell into a specific profile or cluster, one cannot infer that the same percentage of all dechurched people in the United States would be in that same cluster. The goal of phases 2 and 3 was not to acquire a random sample of dechurched individuals but merely to survey a large enough number of the dechurched to conduct this analysis in a statistically rigorous way.

Phase 2 found that no theological tradition, age group, ethnicity, political affiliation, education level, geographic location, or income bracket escaped the dechurching in America. In this phase, we were able to create models for dechurched mainline Christians and dechurched Roman Catholic Christians. We learned that every possible category of people is leaving the church. Yes, some groups of people are leaving faster than others, and some are leaving earlier than others, but all groups and classes of people are experiencing dechurching at historic levels.

Phase 3: What Is Happening in Evangelicalism?

The third phase of our study focused specifically on those who had dechurched from evangelical churches. It included a population size of 2,043 dechurched American adults. As leaders in an evangelical church, we were especially interested in this group. Through the help of machine learning, a branch of artificial intelligence (AI) and computer science that uses algorithms to interpret large quantities of data, we were able to identify four distinct groups of dechurched evangelicals, each with very different animating concerns and each with different paths back. These groups are cultural Christians; dechurched mainstream evangelicals; exvangelicals; and dechurched Black, indigenous, and people of color (BIPOC).

This book is the compilation of our research and our practical pastoral applications to better understand and address the Great Dechurching. An important caveat. We are pastors, not scholars. Our hope is that this intersection between the academy (the research) and the church (our application of the research) will render reliable, helpful, and actionable results for many different expressions of the local church and that scholars in many fields would build on this conversation with their unique skills and experience. Our findings confirmed our grim assumptions about the state of churchgoing in the US today, yet they were also surprisingly hopeful in many ways. All is not lost. In fact, the American church's greatest work may well be ahead.

Part 1

Meet the Dechurched

Chapter 1

What Is at Stake?

IN THE UNITED STATES, WE ARE CURRENTLY EXPERIENCING THE largest and fastest religious shift in the history of our country, as tens of millions of formerly regular Christian worshipers nation-wide have decided they no longer desire to attend church at all. These are what we now call the dechurched. About 40 million adults in America today used to go to church but no longer do, which accounts for around 16 percent[1] of our adult population. For the first time in the eight decades that Gallup has tracked American religious membership, more adults in the United States do not attend church than attend church.[2] This is not a gradual shift; it is a jolting one.

---

1. For the purposes of this book, we are going to say there are 40 million dechurched adult Americans. There were 258.3 million adult Americans in the 2020 census, hence, 15.5 percent of American adults are dechurched.

2. "U.S. Adult Population Grew Faster Than Nation's Total Population from 2010 to 2020," United States Census Bureau, https://www.census.gov/library/stories/2021/08 /united-states-adult-population-grew-faster-than-nations-total-population-from-2010-to -2020.html; and Jeffrey M. Jones, "U.S. Church Membership Falls below Majority for First Time," Gallup, March 29, 2021, https://news.gallup.com/poll/341963/church-membership-falls-below-majority-first-time.aspx.

Historical Context

There have been roughly three periods of rapid growth in religious adherence in the United States: the First Great Awakening (1730s–1740s), the Second Great Awakening (1790–1840), and the four decades following the Civil War (1870–1906).[3] From 1700 to 1776, religious adherence grew in the US from 10 percent to 17 percent. Interestingly enough, and perhaps contrary to popular opinion, "Historians of American religion have long noted that the colonies did not exude universal piety. There was general agreement that in the colonial period no more than 10–20 percent of the population actually belonged to a church."[4] Finke and Stark estimate the national religious adherence rate to be 17 percent in 1776 with 3,228 congregations and an estimated 242,100 members.[5]

Rates of religious adherence rose significantly between 1776 and 1850, from 17 percent to 34 percent, primarily due to the Second Great Awakening that roughly spanned the fifty-year period from 1790 to 1840.[6] Despite this rapid growth, the fastest period of growth in religious adherence was the twenty-five-year period after the Civil War.[7]

From 1870 to 1895, church attendance more than doubled, from 13.5 million people to 32.7 million,[8] as the general population grew from 38.6 million[9] to 69.6 million people.[10] The net result was a

---

3. Accurate data on religious adherence and churching is difficult to find before 1776, but Roger Finke and Rodney Stark have done excellent work in their book *The Churching of America, 1776–2005* (New Brunswick, NJ: Rutgers University Press, 2005).

4. Finke and Stark, 29.

5. Finke and Stark, 29.

6. Finke and Stark, 23.

7. Finke and Stark, 23, fig. 1.2.

8. Finke and Stark, 23, fig. 1.2.

9. "1870 Fast Facts United States," United States Census Bureau, https://www.census.gov/history/www/through_the_decades/fast_facts/1870_fast_facts.html.

10. "1890 Fast Facts United States," United States Census Bureau, https://www.census.gov/history/www/through_the_decades/fast_facts/1890_fast_facts.html; "1900 Fast Facts

12 percent increase in churchgoers.[11] Because this growth happened in the short span of only twenty-five years, it became the largest religious shift in the history of our country until now. What we have witnessed in the last twenty-five years is a religious shift about 1.25 times larger but going in the opposite direction. In that time, about 40 million people have stopped attending church. More people have left the church in the last twenty-five years than all the new people who became Christians from the First Great Awakening, Second Great Awakening, and Billy Graham crusades *combined*.[12] Adding to the alarm is the fact that this phenomenon has rapidly increased since the mid-1990s.

The 1990s is when churchgoing in America really changed. As Ryan Burge writes, "The early 1990s was an inflection point for American religion. Between the early 1970s and 1990s, the share of Americans who had no religious affiliation had only risen two points. But from that point forward, the nones would grow by a percentage point or two nearly every year through the following three decades."[13] Here the term *nones* refers to those with no religious affiliation.

So, what happened? While there is room for nuance on the acceleration of dechurching in the 1990s, three factors cannot be overlooked. First, during the Cold War, the terms *American* and

United States," United States Census Bureau, https://www.census.gov/history/www/through_the_decades/fast_facts/1900_fast_facts.html. Note that the 1895 population is approximated by taking the average of the 1890 and 1900 censuses.

11. Reworking of figure 1.2 as found in Finke and Stark, *Churching of America*, 23.

12. Finke and Stark, 23, fig. 1.2: 17% of US churched in 1776 (First Great Awakening doubled churching, adding some 2.5 million adherents), Second Great Awakening added 10% churched (from 35 to 45% from 1870 to 1890, adding 14.9 million adherents). The worldwide Billy Graham crusades added some 3.2 million people over the course of the Billy Graham crusades, according to Billy Graham Evangelistic Association staff. https://web.archive.org/web/20081203122410/http://cincinnati.com/billygraham/p_man.html.

13. Ryan Burge, "'OK Millennial': Don't Blame the Boomers for Decline of Religion in America," *Religion News Service*, August 30, 2021, https://religionnews.com/2021/08/30/ok-millennial-dont-blame-the-boomers-for-decline-of-religion-in-america/.

Christian were often used synonymously in our struggle against a nation that posed an existential threat to America's way of life. President Ronald Reagan called the Soviet Union "the Evil Empire." During this period, we added "In God We Trust" to our currency and "under God" to our Pledge of Allegiance. When the Soviet Union collapsed and that struggle ended, it became more culturally acceptable to be both American and non-Christian.

Figure 1.1. The Religious Affiliation of 18-to-35-Year-Olds

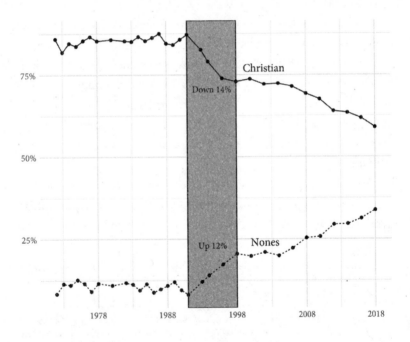

Second, there was fallout from an increasingly polarized religious Right. Under the influence of Jerry Falwell's Moral Majority, Pat Robertson's challenge to the George Bush GOP, and Newt Gingrich's uncompromising takeover of the House, Americans in the middle associated Christianity exclusively with these movements and began to let go of all of it. The formerly religious middle began to join the budding ranks of the nones.

Third, we cannot overstate the influence of the internet in driving the acceleration of dechurching in America. Even though the internet was slow and, according to the Census Bureau,[14] only in 20 percent of American homes by 1997, students had access to the World Wide Web in schools. In 1994 the internet cafe was born, and the first internet connections in public libraries became available. For the first time, people could easily and regularly engage a wide range of worldviews very different from their own and collaborate in communities with others questioning their faith without the risk of social and familial opposition.

The size and scope of this shift away from church is unprecedented in our country. Dechurching is an epidemic and will impact both the institutions of our country and the very fabric of our society within our lifetime. This seismic shift in religious belief and church attendance is a new era in American history we call the Great Dechurching.

An important aim in our study was to find the last time someone attended church more than once per year (fig. 1.2). Whatever the reason (and we will explore those reasons in depth), the numbers were staggering as we realized that most of the dechurching has happened in the last twenty-five years and is accelerating. At some point, the rate of dechurching will slow down, not necessarily because the underlying reasons have been mitigated, but simply because there won't be enough people going to church regularly to sustain the rate of people leaving the church. The dechurched will give way to the unchurched—those who never attended church to begin with.

---

14. Camille Ryan, "Computer and Internet Use in the United States: 2016," United States Census Bureau, August 2018, https://www.census.gov/content/dam/Census/library /publications/2018/acs/ACS-39.pdf.

Figure 1.2. What Year Did You Last Attend a Congregation a Few Times a Year?

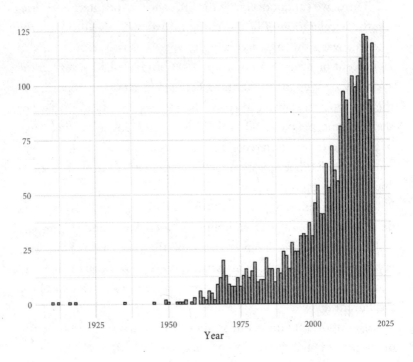

The Stakes

The erosion of the religious foundation of 40 million people will have widespread reverberations. The dechurching implications for America fall into three main categories: what is at stake relationally, religiously, and culturally. With respect to what is at stake relationally, we will look at the toll dechurching is taking on families and friendships. Then we will look at the implications religiously for churches, denominations, and networks. Finally, we will examine what is at stake culturally, looking at the impact of dechurching on communities, culture, and country.

What Is at Stake Relationally: Families and Friendships

The dechurching phenomenon is a tremendous source of pain for many at the familial level. I (Mike) was talking with a woman recently who has four adult children. They all grew up in the church and in Christian schools. This woman is one of the kindest, godliest, and sincerest people I have ever known. She is a fabulous mom and overall person. However, three of her four kids don't go to church and are completely done with Christianity. Imagine her pain.

We have spent countless pastoral hours talking, praying, and agonizing with parents and grandparents who are in anguish over their family members who have left the church. And the more we talk with people over age fifty, the more this dynamic seems to be the norm rather than the exception. Some of these stories include addiction, destructive behaviors, gender and sexual confusion, and even suicide. Anecdotally, we know of almost no parents over the age of fifty who don't have at least one adult child who is dechurched. Many pray for hours each week that God will bring their children or grandchildren to the faith and back to a good church. We've prayed with some parents for their dechurched children for nearly twenty years. We cannot understate the pain, anguish, and grief they face.

On the other hand, relational tension with a parent can often be the cause of a child leaving the church. We learned in our research that 68 percent of dechurched evangelicals said their parents played a role in that decision (see fig. 1.3).

We will spend most of chapter 10, "The Missed Generational Handoff," unpacking what we learned about the dechurched and their relationship with their parent(s), but for now the top five reasons cited in our study were:

1. All their emphasis on culture war lost me over time (14%)
2. Their lack of love, joy, gentleness, kindness, and generosity (14%)

3. Their inability to listen (14%)
4. Their inability to engage with other viewpoints (13%)
5. Their racial attitudes or actions (13%)

Figure 1.3. How Big of an Influence Were Your Parents in Dechurching?

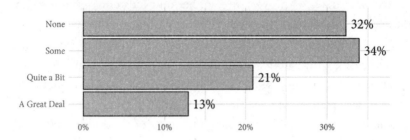

The dechurching phenomenon has become disruptive between multiple generations of family members, causing two-way relational tension between parents (and grandparents) and their adult children that has no quick fix. Among dechurched evangelicals, about two-thirds expressed that their parents' evangelical faith played a role in pushing them away from church. Much of this tension can be summarized by either a difference in political vision or in one's affective posture toward culture and society. The chasm is wider in some profiles than others, and there is a lot of hope in these relationships with growth in relational wisdom. Later in the book, we explore what is going on and to see if there are some best practices to help relieve some of that tension.

Among evangelicals in our study, there is a higher rate of marriage among the dechurched (77%) than there is among people who are still actively churched (62%). Dechurched evangelicals in our study also have a lower rate of divorce at 8 percent compared to 13 percent among still churched evangelicals. One might expect the opposite, but when you read more on the profiles in the coming chapters, you will see that there is quite a bit of complexity to the various profiles. Any good study will produce results that challenge our assumptions and cause us to think with greater depth and nuance about what we are observing.

Dechurching doesn't just impact multiple generations of families; it also has impacted our friendships. Anecdotally, at least half of my (Mike's) friends with whom I grew up and went to church with don't go anymore. More recently people who used to go to church together have just stopped going altogether. This is sad and disappointing, and it leaves us with a lot of complex emotions. We miss these people dearly, and cumulatively their absence is reshaping whole churches, denominations, and networks.

What Is at Stake Religiously: Churches, Denominations, and Networks

For the first time in the Gallup poll's eight-decade history, in 2020 church membership in the United States fell below 50 percent in America.[15] From World War II all the way to the mid-1990s, church membership among adults was nearly always above 70 percent. The precipitous decline occurred across all religious traditions and, as we've already stated, began to pick up steam in the mid-1990s. Membership has dropped by roughly a third across all religious traditions over the last twenty-five years. This invariably has caused more churches to close and has made it more challenging to plant new churches.

According to Lifeway Research, in 2019 approximately 3,000 Protestant churches were started in the US, but 4,500 Protestant

---

15. Jeffrey M. Jones, "U.S. Church Membership Falls Below Majority for First Time," Gallup, March 29, 2021, https://news.gallup.com/poll/341963/church-membership-falls-below -majority-first-time.aspx.

churches closed.[16] Just five years prior, in 2014, the same Lifeway study found that 3,700 churches had closed and 4,000 had opened. As you can see, the rate of church planting has slowed, and the rate of church closures has accelerated. The dechurching phenomenon is likely a large factor in those shifts.

According to the 2020 Faith Communities Today (FACT) study on all kinds of faith communities, "the vast majority of the country's congregations are small. 70% of these faith communities have 100 or fewer weekly attendees. Only 10% of them have more than 250 in weekly services. However, far more people attend these larger congregations—roughly 70% of all attendees–than the many smaller ones."[17] Churches under 100 people comprise 69 percent of all churches. However, 70 percent of all US church attenders go to churches that have 250 or more people.[18] Hence, smaller churches are far more common; however, far more people attend larger churches when you add up the sum total of people in those larger churches. The dechurching phenomenon is likely to hit smaller churches proportionally much harder, and we will likely see more consolidation of churches into medium and larger churches.

If the church closing and planting trends from 2019 continue, we will continue to see the total number of Protestant churches in America decline. As the overall numbers of members in a denomination decline, we are likely to see a drop in financial giving toward the denominations and networks with which these churches belong. This will put strain on denominations, their global missions efforts, their domestic ministries, and their academic and theological institutions.

---

16. Aaron Earls, "Protestant Church Closures Outpace Openings in U.S.," Lifeway Research, May 25, 2021, https://research.lifeway.com/2021/05/25/protestant-church-closures-outpace-openings-in-u-s/.

17. Scott Thumma, "Twenty Years of Congregational Change: The 2020 Faith Communities Today Overview," Hartford Institute for Religious Research, 2021, https://faithcommunitiestoday.org/wp-content/uploads/2021/10/Faith-Communities-Today-2020-Summary-Report.pdf, 5.

18. Thumma, 5, fig. 2.

Figure 1.4. Mainline Protestant Percent of US Population

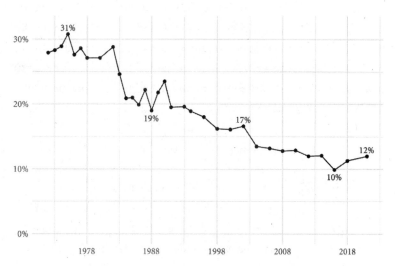

The 40 million Americans who have left houses of worship represent a total annual income of $1.4 trillion dollars.[19] According to Nonprofits Source, the average American Christian gives 2.5 percent of their income.[20] Seventy percent of Americans self-identify as some type of Christian tradition,[21] so that means conceivably $24.7 billion dollars *per year* just left Christian churches. The economic impact of these losses cannot be underestimated and will have implications beyond just individual local churches.

Dechurching has been particularly pronounced in some

---

19. Figure derived from $35,384 per capita income in 2020 times 40 million people. "QuickFacts United States," United States Census Bureau, https://www.census.gov/quickfacts /fact/table/US/SEX255221.

20. "Church and Religious Charitable Giving Statistics," Nonprofits Source, https://nonprofitssource.com/online-giving-statistics/church-giving/.

21. PRRI Staff, "The 2020 Census of American Religion," PRRI, July 8, 2021, https://www.prri.org/research/2020-census-of-american-religion/#:~:text=More%20than%20four%20in%20ten%20(41%25)%20identify%20as%20Protestant,Jewish%2C%20Muslim%2C%20and%20Hindu.

unexpected places such as the secular right (which we will address in chapter 2) and in the Bible Belt. We have seen this both in our study and in the largest and longest religious data study in America, the General Social Survey (GSS). Historian Daniel Williams's analysis of the GSS[22] has shown that this rising secular right is marked by hyper-individualism, law and order, insensitive racial attitudes,[23] cynicism toward institutions, anti-abortion, and libertine positions on sexuality. Williams concludes,

> For decades, many pundits have warned about the political dangers of a Southern Christian Right that was intent on blurring the boundaries of church and state. But whatever those dangers might have been, perhaps the greater threat to democracy in the South right now is a de-churched populist Right that is just as angry about efforts to correct racial injustice and even more individualistic.
>
> Whether we call it "evangelical" or simply "Southern populist," this post-church Southern Protestant Right is not going to go away just because the Southern Baptist Convention loses members. In fact, it's likely to become stronger than ever.[24]

The rise of those dechurching on the secular right will reshape not just the Southern Baptist Convention but all denominations, especially among evangelicals. This dynamic will not just impact churches, denominations, and networks but will also continue to remake communities, culture, and country.

---

22. Daniel K. Williams, "White Southern Evangelicals Are Leaving the Church," *Christianity Today*, August 2, 2022, https://www.christianitytoday.com/ct/2022/august-web-only/church-attendance-sbc-southern-evangelicals-now-lapsed.html.

23. Williams. "They opposed 'preferential hiring' for Blacks by a margin of more than 4 to 1. Likewise, by a margin of more than 4 to 1, they agreed with this statement: 'Irish, Italians, Jewish, and many other minorities overcame prejudice and worked their way up. Blacks should do the same.' When asked why Blacks, on average, had 'worse jobs, income, and housing than white people,' nearly half said it was because they 'just don't have the motivation or willpower to pull themselves out of poverty.'"

24. Williams.

RYAN BURGE: One of the primary lenses through which demographers can track religious decline is through denominational records. Almost every large religious tradition has been tracking their total membership for decades as a means of understanding where churches are growing and where they are declining. Anyone who has been in church administration for a while knows that membership records are far from accurate. Churches don't want to cull people from the rolls because there's always the possibility that they will return to church one day and express offense when seeing that their name has been purged from the official records. However, despite their drawbacks, denominational records are still one of the best data sources that exist when it comes to tracking the growth or decline of American religion.

The portrait they paint is not a rosy one. For instance, in 1990 the Evangelical Lutheran Church in America reported 5.25 million members. In 2020 the total membership was just over 3 million—a decline of 41 percent. The Presbyterian Church (USA) has seen its membership drop 58 percent during the same time period. The United Church of Christ is down 52 percent, and the United Methodist Church has seen a decline of 31 percent. The Episcopal Church, which used to be one of the most influential denominations in the United States, has just half a million people in the pews on an average Sunday and just 1.5 million members total.

This trend is not relegated to mainline traditions alone. The Southern Baptist Convention (SBC), which is the largest evangelical denomination in the United States, has also seen a serious decline in membership in recent years. In 2006, 16.2 million people aligned with the SBC; now that number is 13.7 million. Between 2020 and 2021, the SBC lost nearly 410,000 members. That's the largest single-year loss in the 170 years of the Southern Baptist Convention.

There are two bright spots when it comes to membership. The Assemblies of God, an evangelical denomination with ties to the Pentecostal tradition, has seen their membership numbers rise 50 percent over the last three decades. They also enjoy a high level of racial diversity, while many other Protestant traditions are still overwhelmingly white. The other area seeing positive growth is nondenominational Protestant Christianity. While it's impossible to collect membership statistics on these types of churches, on surveys the portion of Americans who identify as nondenominational rose over the last decade while other traditions like Baptist, Methodist, and Lutheran have all declined.

What Is at Stake Culturally: Communities, Culture, and Country

Healthy communities have economies, laws, organizations, and institutions that, by and large, work for all the members of that community. A quick scroll through social media or stroll past strongly worded neighborhood yard signs in some communities will reveal the obvious: American culture and society are not just polarizing, but fracturing.[25] We've seen protests of all sorts, digital vitriol, uptick in conspiratorial rhetoric, and all sorts of cultural events with widely diverging opinions from the same event. One such national Rorschach test was January 6, 2021, where large portions of the country see treasonous domestic terrorists attacking the nation's seat of power and threatening the life of our second-highest ranking

---

25. "Political Polarization in the American Public," Pew Research Center, June 12, 2014, https://www.pewresearch.org/politics/2014/06/12/political-polarization-in-the-american-public/.

official, whereas another large part of the country sees American patriots defending the Constitution. It is hard not to look at such divergence and conclude that the country has serious problems it has to address.

The country is increasingly partisan and politically polarized. It used to be that median Democrats and median Republicans weren't that far apart ideologically on political values. Now, however, the gap between them has widened considerably, causing significant erosion of centrist Americans.[26] This dynamic has complex roots, but it's clear that there is also a decreased trust in a wide array of institutions. Further, only 25 percent of Americans now place their trust in other Americans.[27]

We don't know anyone who hasn't lost friends over the last few years. To maintain friendship in real life or online, it feels like people must agree with you on whole new lists of things that we didn't have in the past. Some of those new litmus tests might be wise, but some can be quite unhealthy. If someone is saying racist or cruel things on the internet or in real life, then wisdom probably merits some relational boundaries. However, maybe it isn't the best idea to end relationships over viewpoints on climate change, gun control, or a whole host of other matters.

It only makes sense that the fracturing of American culture and society and the erosion of American institutions it has caused would spill over into the pews. *Christianity Today* CEO, Tim Dalrymple, noted the following:

> New fractures are forming within the American evangelical movement, fractures that do not run along the usual regional,

---

26. Lee Rainie and Andrew Perrin, "Key Findings about Americans' Declining Trust in Government and Each Other," Pew Research Center, July 22, 2019, https://www.pewresearch.org/fact-tank/2019/07/22/key-findings-about-americans-declining-trust-in-government-and-each-other/.

27. Rainie and Perrin.

denominational, ethnic, or political lines. Couples, families, friends, and congregations once united in their commitment to Christ are now dividing over seemingly irreconcilable views of the world. In fact, they are not merely dividing but becoming incomprehensible to one another.[28]

Cultural, sociological, ideological, and experiential factors are rapidly and radically sorting American culture and society. Consider the wide varieties of opinions among the people in your life regarding Donald Trump, January 6, George Floyd, Black Lives Matter, COVID-19, gun control, #ChurchToo, and #MeToo.

Christianity Today editor-in-chief Russell Moore put it this way:

> In many of these [formerly religious] places, to be a grown-up and not a rebel or weirdo meant you attended church. Yet increasingly, I once argued, it was less and less necessary for people to go to church for those cultural reasons.
>
> What I didn't count on was that cultural Christianity would be infected with a delta variant and morph into something else.
>
> The kind of cultural Christianity we now see often keeps everything about the Religious Right except the religion. These people aren't in Sunday school, but they might post Bible verses on Facebook (or quote them on TikTok).[29]

The same is true for those running for office. To get votes, you need to appeal to the evolving religious Right that looks increasingly more like civil religion than it does gospel religion. Going to church used to confer positive social capital, especially in the Bible Belt, but

28. Timothy Dalrymple, "The Splintering of the Evangelical Soul," *Christianity Today*, April 16, 2021, https://www.christianitytoday.com/ct/2021/april-web-only/splintering-of -evangelical-soul.html.
29. Russell Moore, "When the South Loosens Its Bible Belt," *Christianity Today*, August 11, 2022, https://www.christianitytoday.com/ct/2022/august-web-only/russell-moore-white -evangelicals-bible-belt-south-church.html.

increasingly what is imputing positive social capital is mirroring the political civil religion of your immediate physical context and the makeup of your digital community. That knife cuts both ways politically. If you are in a blue city, state, or digital ecosystem, then you need to say certain things to maintain thick social ties. In our current situation, that might look like expressing sentiments around politics, policy, gender, sexuality, or race. This is simply the logical outcome of an increasingly polarized America.[30]

When we consider what is happening in families, friendships, and communities, it isn't hard to trace a trajectory for the country. More cultural fracturing, more privatization, erosion of institutions, loss of public trust, and thinner communities. Even if you have no faith whatsoever, a case can be made that dechurching is impacting you, your community, and your country negatively. Consider the fact that nearly all hospitals and orphanages in America were religiously founded to promote well-being in culture and society. A similar thing can be said for many of our country's earliest universities and educational institutions. One study notes that religiously affiliated nonprofits comprise 40 percent of the social safety net in America.[31]

Dechurching will invariably diminish resources that provide relief, care, and aid to the poor, disenfranchised, sick, hurting, and otherwise needy. Further, increasing atomization and retreat into our digital selves putting additional strain on the societal fabric.

It is impossible for 40 million American adults leaving their former houses of worship not to reshape communities across the country. Some will be impacted by long-standing churches closing

---

30. "As Partisan Hostility Grows, Signs of Frustration with the Two-Party System," Pew Research Center, August 9, 2022, https://www.pewresearch.org/politics/2022/08/09/as -partisan-hostility-grows-signs-of-frustration-with-the-two-party-system/.

31. "Faith-Inspired Nonprofits Provide 40 Percent of Social Safety Net Spending but Can Still Be Overlooked by Donors, according to New Bridgespan Group Research," Bridgespan Group, January 28, 2021, https://www.bridgespan.org/about-us/for-the-media/faith -inspired-nonprofits-provide-40-percent-of-so#:~:text=Reality%3A%20Data%20from%20 Giving%20USA,nongovernmental%20organizations%20are%20faith%2Dinspired.

their doors. Others will experience churches with diminished capacity to do good works. The fabric of those communities will be weaker if the connective-tissue role that churches often play becomes more hardened and sclerotic. Many studies have shown that vibrant faith communities often provide tremendous benefit to the broader community.[32]

The net result of dechurching could be diminished human flourishing, connectivity, cohesiveness, and overall shalom.

Reason for Hope

While the situation is bleak, there is plenty of reason for hope. We want to see our friends, family, and people in our community return to church so we can build better cities around the kind of human flourishing that derives from a robust gospel. The goal isn't to make us a Christian nation but to see how Christians impact the culture we live in. The keys to addressing the Great Dechurching will be whether churchgoing people will be willing to seek understanding, relate with wisdom, build healthier institutions, embrace our exilic nature, and seek a gospel that is true, good, and beautiful. In the next chapter, we will look at the high-altitude observations from our study on who the dechurched are and draw some initial ministry implications.

---

32. Tyler J. VanderWeele, "Religious Communities and Human Flourishing," *Current Directions in Psychological Science* 26, no. 5 (October 2017): 476–81, https://pubmed.ncbi.nlm.nih.gov/29170606/.

Chapter 2

Who Are the Dechurched?

TO ADEQUATELY ADDRESS THE GREAT DECHURCHING, WE MUST first understand who is leaving and why. Some have suggested that what would have naturally happened in many social realms over the next ten to fifteen years was accelerated by the recent political, racial, and pandemic turmoil. Carlos Lozada, in a 2020 *Washington Post* article, reported, "The virus isn't transforming us. It's speeding up the changes already underway."[1]

Others have suggested that as our culture becomes less accommodating and even hostile to the Christian faith, we simply get a clearer picture of who is really committed to that faith in a sort of purification of the church. Thomas Kidd, author and research professor at Midwestern Baptist Theological Seminary, writes, "We're not so much concerned with 'mere' church members, but 'regenerate' church members."[2]

---

1. Carlos Lozada, "The Great Acceleration," *Washington Post*, December 18, 2020, https://www.washingtonpost.com/outlook/2020/12/18/coronavirus-great-acceleration-changes-society/.
2. Thomas Kidd, "Why American Church Membership Is Plummeting," TGC, April 1,

Still others claim we are doing this to ourselves. A May 2022 article in *The Atlantic* claims, "The movement [that] spent 40 years at war with secular America [is] now at war with itself,"[3] and the result is a fracturing of the American church.[4] Who is correct? The data from our survey suggest they all might be.

Dechurching Is Happening Everywhere

No group of people is immune from the Great Dechurching. The dechurched are almost evenly split between men and women (52 percent and 48 percent respectively). According to our study, Roman Catholics, Protestants, and those who identify as "other Christian" have all dechurched equally at 32 percent. In the Protestant tradition, Presbyterians lead the dechurching, losing about 45 percent of their attenders over the last twenty-five years. This is largely due to dechurching in the mainline Presbyterian Church (PCUSA). Methodists follow at 37 percent, Baptists at 29 percent, and Pentecostals at 26 percent.

By generation, the baby boomers (those born between 1946 and 1964) are dechurching in larger numbers as more than 35 percent of the boomers living today have stopped attending church. This is about twice the size of millennials (between 17% and 25%), which is not a surprise as more baby boomers went to church in the first place, which gives them more opportunity to make this shift. Black

2021, https://www.thegospelcoalition.org/blogs/evangelical-history/why-americas-church
-membership-rate-is-cratering/.

3. Tim Alberta, "How Politics Poisoned the Evangelical Church," *Atlantic*, May 10, 2022, https://www.theatlantic.com/magazine/archive/2022/06/evangelical-church-pastors
-political-radicalization/629631/.

4. Michael Graham with Skyler Flowers, "The Six Way Fracturing of Evangelicalism," *Mere Orthodoxy*, June 7, 2021, https://mereorthodoxy.com/six-way-fracturing-evangelicalism/.

and white Americans are dechurching in comparable numbers (26% and 27% respectively). Hispanic Americans are experiencing the least dechurching at 14 percent, and somewhat perplexingly, 34 percent of Asian Americans have dechurched.[5]

Unsurprisingly, sexual orientation is a strong indicator of church attendance. According to the 2020 Cooperative Election Study at Harvard University, a heterosexual man is almost three times as likely to attend church at least once a year than a gay man. A heterosexual woman is one and a half times more likely to attend church at least once a year than a gay woman or anyone who identifies as bisexual. While our study did not focus on dechurched LGBTQ+ people, they were included in the study, and we can at least say that they left for different reasons. Some left because they felt the church was too restrictive of their sexual freedom, but others left because they didn't feel like they were welcome, often because their churches either didn't adequately address the issue or addressed it in a harsh and insensitive manner.

Figure 2.1. Religious Service Attendance by Sexual Orientation

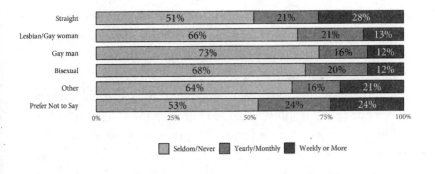

---

5. Without a deep dive into Asian American dechurching, we cannot empirically say why they are dechurching so fast. This is an area that warrants further study.

Neither the political left nor the right is immune to the religious shifts of our day. Twenty-one percent of those who identify as Republican, 23 percent of those who identify as Independent, and 29 percent of those who identify as Democrat and used to go to church have stopped. Americans at every income level, educational status, and area of the country are deciding to forgo their in-person worship for other activities on Sunday morning.

Not Everyone Is Leaving for the Same Reasons

It quickly became clear that we can't lump all the dechurched into the same category when it comes to the animating concerns behind their decision to stop attending. One large group stopped attending church without initially intending to do so. Some moved to a new city with the intention of finding a church but never took that next step into a faith community. Many young professionals prioritized personal networks around their careers and, as a result, found themselves disconnected from a local church. Some families prioritized children's sports and other activities that increasingly happen on Sundays. Then there are those who stopped attending church during COVID-19. They developed new Sunday rhythms and now prefer those new activities over Sunday morning worship. We call all this group the casually dechurched.

Others, though, experienced genuine pain that led them to lose hope in the institution of the church or the Christian faith altogether. The list of these points of trauma and frustration is long, but it includes spiritual and physical abuse in the church, hypocrisy among church members and leaders, sexual ethics, political syncretism, political disagreement, suffering, racism, bigotry, and a perceived lack of relevance or real answers to the world's problems. Some in this group are victims of pastoral malpractice, and some are victims of the draw of the world and the flesh. We call this group the dechurched casualties.[6]

Education and Income Levels Subvert Expectations

In every tradition, the more education people have, the more likely they are to stay in church. This offers a surprising challenge to the common belief that higher education is facilitating departures from the church. Many Christian colleges were founded based on the belief that secular liberal arts colleges and institutions of higher education lead young Christians astray. For example, the founder of Bob Jones University said, "Bob Jones College . . . stands for the narrow road. We don't stand for the broad road. We don't stand for what is stood for in most educational institutions."[7] While the value of Christian versus secular higher education is a complex topic beyond the scope of this book, support for the idea that secular higher education has a negative effect on the Christian faith may not be as well-founded as many assume. In fact, the opposite may be true.

Ryan Burge wrote on this phenomenon in *The Wall Street Journal*:

It pains me to say that I don't have much influence over the students in my courses. But that doesn't mean college doesn't change them. Looked at in its entirety, the college experience may actually make students more sure of their religious beliefs after they graduate. This is the idea known to psychologists as the "inoculation effect": When someone is confronted with weak attacks on their beliefs, they become more prepared to defend those beliefs

---

6. Credit Skyler Flowers, associate pastor, Grace Bible Church, Oxford, Mississippi, for the terms "casually dechurched" and "dechurched casualties."

7. Bob Jones Sr., *Things I Have Learned: Chapel Talks* (Greenville, SC: Bob Jones University Press), 75–76.

when they come under serious attacks. This is essentially how a vaccine works: It gives an individual a weakened version of the virus, so that when the immune system encounters the real thing, it can easily fight off the villain. Similarly, challenging a young person to defend their beliefs in a supportive, open environment like college may leave them better prepared to hold firm to their convictions later in life.[8]

The data also leads us to believe that the more educated a person is, the more likely they are to see social value in religion, believe in institutions, and have higher levels of interpersonal trust.[9]

Broadly speaking, and contrary to modern sociological opinion that Christianity is more attractive to the poor, our research overwhelmingly shows that Americans who make less money are more likely to dechurch than those who make more money. Why is this the case? In our opinion, America is largely built for a specific type of person. If you belong to a nuclear family, graduate from college, and have children after marriage, America's institutions tend to work better for you. If you get off that track (or never started on it), the US is a more difficult place in which to thrive. Ninety-seven percent of millennial Americans live above the poverty level if they follow what American Enterprise Institute calls the *success sequence*,[10] which involves three things: graduating from high school, working full-time, and having children after you get married. The more you get out of that success sequence, the more the friction between you and American institutions increases. The church is no exception to that. We cannot underestimate the real challenges often posed when there

8. Ryan Burge, "There's No Crisis of Faith on Campus," *Wall Street Journal*, February 24, 2022, https://www.wsj.com/articles/theres-no-crisis-of-faith-on-campus-11645714717.

9. Burge addresses this issue in more depth in his book *20 Myths about Religion and Politics in America* (Minneapolis: Fortress, 2022).

10. W. Bradford Wilcox and Wendy Wang, "The Power of the Success Sequence," American Enterprise Institute, May 26, 2022, https://www.aei.org/research-products/report/the-power-of-the-success-sequence.

is friction from differences in class, race, education, marital status, employment type, or nonnuclear family.

The American church and especially evangelicalism is largely built for the nuclear family or those on that track. The young, single parent working multiple jobs to make ends meet is going to find it harder to create the bandwidth necessary for meaningful church involvement and be more likely to experience depression and even shame in a church culture that creates programs that work for and elevate the nuclear family. The early church that used to cheerfully bring the poor and destitute into their lives now (at least in the US) often serves them at a distance through benevolence programs without fully embracing them into their church family. Modern American churches are financially incentivized to target the wealthy and create a space where those on track feel comfortable. Biblical hospitality, though, is so much more than just throwing money at a problem, and the net result is that the average American church is not truly hospitable to the less fortunate, making them feel like outsiders in our midst.

Dechurched Evangelicals Are Largely Still Orthodox

The part of our study concerning dechurched evangelicals provided possibly the biggest surprise and the most hope. Dechurched evangelicals are still largely orthodox in their faith. When it comes to our primary doctrines, 68 percent of those we surveyed still believe in the Trinity, 64 percent believe in the divinity of Jesus, 65 percent believe Jesus' death on the cross paid the penalty for the sins of those who believe in him, 67 percent believe in the resurrection, 62 percent believe that Jesus is the only way to God, and 61 percent believe the Bible is a reliable document for all matters of faith and practice. Collectively, the general orthodoxy scores of dechurched evangelicals in our study are much higher than their mainline or Roman Catholic counterparts. While they may have departed from the church, their responses indicate that they may not have departed from the faith.

When we focused on why this group of people left the church and how they thought they would come back, the answer was simple: belonging. Sociologists have long divided sociology of religion into the categories of believing, belonging, and behaving (categories we will expand on in later chapters). The animating concerns for their departures and potential return mainly fall into the category of belonging. When asked why they stopped attending a house of worship, 19 percent said they moved and didn't find a new faith community, 14 percent said they didn't experience much love from their faith community, 14 percent said they didn't fit in, 13 percent said that COVID-19 got them out of the habit, 12 percent said their friends weren't attending with them, and 13 percent said that recent family changes like divorce or remarriage made church feel uncomfortable.

When asked how willing they would be to go back to church, 51 percent said they are either somewhat willing or very willing—51 percent! Unsurprisingly, the reasons they would come back also represent a longing to belong. These dechurched evangelicals said they would come back if they made new friends (28%), if they move and want to make new friends (18%), if they became lonely and want to make new friends (20%), if their children want to go (16%), if their spouse wants to go (18%), if a friend invites them (17%), if there is a good pastor (18%), if they find a good community (17%), if they miss their church community (20%), or if they just find a church they like (14%). This group's high orthodoxy scores also inform other reasons they would come back: if they feel the distance from God (20%) or if God tells them to go back in some significant way (18%).

The main takeaway here is that many dechurched evangelicals simply need a friend to invite them to church. For hundreds of thousands of dechurched evangelical Christians, all they need is a personal invitation to a decent church community. We gave our early research to a Presbyterian (EPC) church called The Crossing in Columbia, Missouri, and they began initiatives to engage this group of people. Some initiatives were technology based and some were more personal. They identified dechurched evangelicals whose dechurching was belonging based, and in just a matter of months, they had over 120 formerly dechurched people worshiping with them in person! The Great Dechurching is reversible and doesn't have to have the final word for faith communities in our country.

Mental Health Is an Issue

In phase 3 of our study, we looked at the mental health of dechurched evangelicals, and it became clear that anxiety, depression, loneliness, and suicidal thoughts were major factors in their lives. When asked to rate themselves on a scale of 0–100 in these areas, with 0 being very negative and unhealthy and 100 being very positive and healthy, they scored 39 on anxiety, 34 on depression, 35 on loneliness, and 25 on suicidal thoughts.

There is strong scientific evidence that supports the correlation between church attendance and improved physical and mental health. Tyler VanderWeele, a professor of epidemiology in the Departments of Epidemiology and Biostatistics at Harvard University, has conducted some of the largest studies ever on the role of religious attendance along with colleagues at the Human Flourishing Program at Harvard. Tyler and his team concluded that "compared with those who never attended religious services, individuals who attended services at least once per week had a lower risk of all-cause mortality by 26%, heavy drinking by 34%, and current smoking by 29%."[11] Their

---

11. Ying Chen, Eric S. Kim, and Tyler J. VanderWeele, "Religious-Service Attendance

writing continues to note that "service attendance was also inversely associated with a number of psychological-distress outcomes (i.e. depression, anxiety, hopelessness, loneliness) and was positively associated with psychosocial well-being outcomes (i.e. positive affect, life satisfaction, social integration, purpose in life), but was generally not associated with subsequent disease, such as hypertension, stroke, and heart disease."

Another 2016 study from the same Human Flourishing Program at Harvard of 74,534 women concluded that "frequent attendance at religious services was associated with significantly lower risk of all-cause, cardiovascular, and cancer mortality among women. Religion and spirituality may be an underappreciated resource that physicians could explore with their patients."[12]

The mental health picture we saw in our study was sad for the dechurched, showing such low self-reported figures on anxiety, depression, loneliness, and suicidal thoughts. There is no doubt that the underlying reasons for these numbers are varied and complex, but there does seem to be strong scientific evidence that regular, especially weekly, church attendance is good for your mental and physical health.

The Secular Right Is Dechurching Too

Secularism is likely not a new concept to most Americans today. For centuries the Western world has increasingly made major life decisions based on what we can see and touch in our temporal lives

and Subsequent Health and Well-Being Throughout Adulthood: Evidence from Three Prospective Cohorts," *International Journal of Epidemiology* 49, no. 6 (December 2020): 2030–40, https://doi.org/10.1093/ije/dyaa120.

12. S. Li, M. J. Stampfer, D. R. Williams, and T. J. VanderWeele, "Association of Religious Service Attendance with Mortality among Women," *JAMA Intern Med* 176, no. 6 (2016): 777–85, doi:10.1001/jamainternmed.2016.1615.

instead of on the eternal, supernatural claims of the Bible. The secular left is where most American Christians might expect to see dechurching, as those on the secular left tend to be more vocally opposed to Christianity, and their dechurching began some decades ago. But we find the effect of secularism on both the political left and the right. We often hear people attributing the loss of religious adherence solely to "the left," "liberalism," and "progressive" ideology, and while it is true that the secular left has been a source of erosion for congregations, a new secular right is on the rise with a strong focus on nationalism, individualism, law and order, immigration fears, and populist right-wing ideas.[13]

Particularly among evangelicals, there is more danger of dechurching on the right than on the left. In phase 2 of our study, we saw evangelicals dechurching on the political right at twice the frequency of those on the political left, almost catching up to the total percentage of those who have dechurched to the secular left. Neither the secular left nor right is immune to the Great Dechurching. This dynamic has been corroborated by other large studies like the Cooperative Congressional Election Study from 2008 to 2021, where the share of self-identified evangelical Republicans who seldom or never attend church has risen from about 12 percent to 27 percent in just thirteen years.[14]

In our research, 12 percent of the dechurched evangelicals we surveyed said that a disagreement in politics with the clergy was a factor in their departure, and 12 percent also said that a disagreement in politics with the larger congregation contributed to their decision

---

13. Daniel K. Williams, "White Southern Evangelicals Are Leaving the Church," *Christianity Today*, August 2, 2022, https://www.christianitytoday.com/ct/2022/august-web -only/church-attendance-sbc-southern-evangelicals-now-lapsed.html.

14. Ryan Burge (@ryanburge), "Two thirds of evangelicals Republicans reported attending church once a week or more in 2008. It's a bare majority now - 51%. More than once a week attendance has dropped nearly in half - 32% to 18%. 12% attended less than once a year in 2008. It's 27% now," Twitter, 1:24 p.m. February 13, 2023, 1:24 p.m., https://twitter.com /ryanburge/status/1625199296206278671.

Figure 2.2. Share Who Identify as Republican among Never or Seldom Attenders

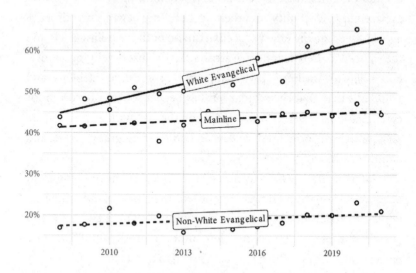

Data from Stephen Ansolabehere, Brian F. Schaffner, and Sam Luks, Cooperative Congressional Election Study, Harvard University, http://cces.gov.harvard.edu. Visualization by Ryan Burge.

to dechurch. For those who indicated that politics was a factor, they also indicated that it was a significant factor. When asked to indicate on a scale of 0–100 how strongly this issue contributed to their dechurching, they responded 53/100 and 64/100 respectively.

This syncretism has two kinds of casualties. There are those who become disenfranchised with the church because it is too synchronized with right-wing politics and those who become disenfranchised with the church because it is not synchronized enough. This is supported in our research, as 28 percent of the dechurched evangelicals we surveyed believe that the United States should be declared a Christian nation and that the success of the United States is part of God's plan for the world. Let that sink in a bit. More than one-quarter of the dechurched evangelicals in our survey believe the

United States should be declared a Christian nation *and* no longer attend church. Among this group of people, the United States is viewed as enjoying special favor with God similar to Israel in the Old Testament. Many believe the US Constitution is divinely inspired, on par with the Bible itself. According to a Pew Research study in 2021,[15] nearly one in five Americans believes the Constitution to be a divinely inspired document. It does not seem like a stretch to conclude that this group has a higher commitment to God's work in the political realm than God's work in his church.

While acknowledging the great blessings we experience in the United States, we as a church need to embrace and display that we have a greater citizenship that transcends our political views and national identity. The issue at hand is a discipleship issue. America is changing, and this creates fear in many because at some level, all change involves loss. It should not surprise us that people are either consciously or subconsciously putting their ultimate hope in the secular right to fix the loss they feel in society. As church leaders, it is our calling to minister to people who are experiencing loss of any kind by pointing them to Jesus, who is the only sure hope in this life and the next.

The Situation Is Urgent

Not only is the scope of dechurching large; the need to engage the dechurched is urgent. In just a generation, the children of the dechurched will be unchurched, changing the nature of spirituality in America significantly. The Pinetops Foundation projects that "even in the most optimistic scenarios, Christian affiliation in the US shrinks dramatically, and in [their] base case, over 1 million youth at

---

15. "In U.S., Far More Support Than Oppose Separation of Church and State," Pew Research Center, October 28, 2021, https://www.pewresearch.org/religion/2021/10/28/in-u-s-far-more-support-than-oppose-separation-of-church-and-state.

least nominally in the church today will choose to leave each year for the next three decades. 35 million youth raised in families that call themselves Christians will say they are not by 2050."[16]

While the term *dechurching* at an academic level goes back to at least the early 1990s, the awareness of this cultural transition is woefully unacknowledged in our general population. As we write this book, the word *dechurched* isn't even recognized by Google Docs or Microsoft Word, which want to change it to *unchurched*. Most churches in America are not equipped to engage those who have left the church or in many cases even retain the people we have.

As church leaders, we believe the Great Dechurching is important because we are talking about real people with eternal souls. In the next five chapters, we will provide profiles of our data that highlight four different types of dechurched evangelicals along with a profile combining mainline and Roman Catholic dechurched individuals. Each will include a fictionalized portrait of someone who might fit that description. The goal of these next five chapters is to give us categories to understand which type of dechurched person we are looking at because they have different reasons for leaving and different paths back. You will learn who these people are and that the majority of dechurched individuals remain interested in spiritual things and are willing to return.

RYAN BURGE: It's hard to fully grasp just how much different American's behavior is around church attendance today versus fifty years ago. The General Social Survey (GSS) is the gold standard for measuring religious changes in the United States. It has been asking the same questions with the same response options since 1972. In the very first administration of the GSS,

---

16. Joshua Crossman, "The Great Opportunity," Pinetops Foundation, September 2017, https://www.greatopportunity.org/.

only 9 percent of respondents said they never attended religious services. Another 8 percent said their attendance was less than once a year. Compare that to 2021, when 31 percent of Americans described their attendance as "never" and another 15 percent said they attended less than yearly. Seventeen percent of people were less than yearly attenders in 1972, but that's nearly half of the population today.

At the same time, the percentage of people who described their attendance as nearly every week or more was 41 percent in 1972. In 2021 that had dropped to just 24 percent. Consider this: In 2021 a person was twice as likely to say their church attendance was less than once a year than they were to report that they attended religious services nearly every week or more. Among those ages 18 to 30, 55 percent attended less than yearly while only 18 percent attended nearly every week.

Speaking from a purely statistical perspective, the future of the American church looks bleak. In the 1970s, pastors and denominational leaders could look across the pews on a Sunday morning and see a lot of young families because nearly a third of young people were faithfully attending. That share has been cut in half now. It won't happen all at once, but slowly over time there will be a few more empty seats every Easter, and the parking lot won't be as packed on Christmas Eve. This will lead church leaders to completely rethink things like budgets, buildings, and staffing levels to adjust to the smaller congregations they are serving.

Part 2

Profiles of the Dechurched

Chapter 3

Cultural Christians

TOM APPROACHED HIS WORKSPACE AT YAHOO FOR THE LAST TIME. He picked up the photo of his wife, Jenny, and the kids at the beach. The new job at Google would open doors for him professionally and provide the income to finally make some of their dreams a reality. Sunnyvale wasn't that far from Palo Alto, but it would mean a far better lifestyle for them, with a bigger house and better schools.

The intercom jolted Tom back into the present. "Someone by the name of Rex is on line two," the receptionist reported. "Says he's a friend of yours?"

"What? You've got to be kidding me!" Tom plopped into his chair and rolled to the right, grabbing the receiver and punching the second button. "Rex? You there?"

"Hey man, what's up?" His old friend's easygoing demeanor hadn't changed a bit. "Long time no see!"

"Too long, my friend. Way too long. I can't believe you caught me here. It's my last day!"

"Well, I've been meaning to look you up for forever, and your online profile showed this as your workplace, so I decided to take a chance."

The two former teammates spent half an hour catching up and

reminiscing about their days at USC. Tom had arrived in LA as an incoming freshman not knowing a soul, so he had just put all his focus on getting good grades and being in peak condition for the upcoming season. Rex was a junior that year and a veteran pitcher. He noticed Tom's blue collar work ethic and decided to take him under his wing.

Rex was a strong Christian and student leader at Fellowship of Christian Athletes. He invited Tom to their meetings and to the large church he attended. It was different from what Tom was used to back in Ohio, but there was enough overlap for him to soon feel comfortable. Being there with Rex made him more confident and a lot less homesick. The two became like brothers, and for the next two years, Tom roomed with Rex in his condo just off campus.

Things had gone well for Tom in those first couple of years at USC. It was the best time of his life. His sophomore season, they were conference champs, with Rex as their starting pitcher and team captain. Miraculously, they won both the regional and super regional tournaments. Going to the College World Series in Omaha was a literal dream come true, even though they ended up losing.

"So are you guys going to try to find a new church closer to Palo Alto?" Rex asked him as the conversation was winding down.

"Well, ah . . . ," Tom hesitated. "We haven't been going anywhere in particular, and with the new job and new schools and all, life is going to be kind of crazy for a while."

"Okay, I get you," Rex affirmed. "Maybe after things settle down a bit. It can really make a difference, you know. Be good for the kids too."

Tom redirected the conversation and brought it to a close. He loved talking to his old friend, but it also brought up a lot of conflicted feelings. As much as he had enjoyed that period of his life, those idyllic times were long gone now, much like his major league dreams.

The week after that College World Series loss was when his life had started going downhill. His dad, Bill, suffered an accident on the automobile production line at work. That July, Rex was drafted by the New York Mets, and Tom lost his best friend, roommate, and living situation. Tom's anxiety mounted. As best he could pinpoint, that was when he began to sink into a season of depression.

Senior year was basically a blur of alcohol, baseball, and differential equations.

Tom tore his rotator cuff in his pitching arm at the end of April. His dreams of being drafted slipped through his fingers.

After he blew out his shoulder, Tom only went to church and FCA about once a month, whenever his depression got bad. He'd once felt almost invincible, like God was with him, but now he felt distant. Doubts crept into Tom's mind about God's goodness and maybe even his existence.

His parents came to visit him to check on him, and that was met with some trepidation.

Tom's parents were union Democrats until Trump. He didn't care for it but understood why his parents supported January 6 and the whole nine yards. He leaned further left on several social and ethical issues, while his parents' faith and politics sort of merged together.

Mainly, Tom was frustrated because he felt his parents wouldn't even listen to his viewpoints anymore. An attitude of cynicism had replaced some of their former openness. Still, he was grateful for everything they had sacrificed to give him a shot at a better life than their own.

Tom and Jenny were looking forward to their next chapter. Jenny was excited about all the things she wanted them to do together as a family now that they would have some expendable income. Her enthusiasm was contagious, as usual.

"Kirsten said we definitely need to go hiking in Muir Woods," she told him. "And, of course, we need to take the kids to see the Giant Sequoias. When they're a little older, we could go sailing at Tahoe or kayaking at La Jolla."

And maybe I can get in a round at Pebble Beach if there's any time left over, Tom hoped to himself.

Getting ready for bed that night, both of them tired from their evening at the parks and rec fields, Jenny rubbed Tom's sore shoulder. "Oh, you never told me about your conversation with Rex! How's he doing?"

"He asked me about church," he sighed. "I don't know, something about this move and talking to him has gotten me thinking about the past versus where I'm at right now." Tom spoke softly, searching for words. "I know you've said in the past that you'd like for us to go to church, and I admit I always wanted that happiness I saw in Rex. It's part of why I was drawn to him as a friend, and when we hung out, I always kind of felt it too." *Then again, if I'd had it as good as he did, I might be more inclined to worship God too.*

Tom rolled over, "But, I mean, just on a practical level, I don't see how we could possibly fit another activity in our family calendar," he reasoned. "Sundays are our only day to spend time at home, relaxing together. Church just isn't a priority for me. I'm not sure it ever will be again."

Understanding Cultural Christians

Tom is a cultural Christian, a demographic pattern we identified in our data that represents the largest of the four subgroups of dechurched evangelicals.[1] It describes a whopping 52 percent of all dechurched evangelicals in our survey. There could be roughly 8 million adult Americans with similar attitudes as Tom's.

Tom's attitude regarding Jesus is one of apathy with a hint of nostalgia. By worldly standards, what else does Tom need? He has

---

1. For more information on study design, sample size, and other types of information please see the introduction.

a wife, kids, good friends, an expensive house, a career, nice things, and vacations. The inertia of life, kids, and high-powered work grinds on. Tom keeps working hard and playing hard. With Tom's story in mind, let's look at what our study discovered about this first and largest group of people who no longer attend church.

Doctrine

We refer to these dechurched Americans as cultural Christians because few of them show much evidence that they are actually believers. Only 1 percent in our survey embrace the truth that "Jesus is the Son of God," and just 22 percent believe "the Bible is the literal Word of God."

Our friend Tom is on the lower end of the orthodoxy score. When we talk orthodoxy throughout the book, we have in view the bare essentials of the faith best outlined in the Nicene Creed:

I believe in one God, the Father Almighty, Maker of heaven and earth, and of all things visible and invisible.

And in one Lord Jesus Christ, the only-begotten Son of God, begotten of the Father before all worlds; God of God, Light of Light, very God of very God; begotten, not made, being of one substance with the Father, by whom all things were made.

Who, for us men for our salvation, came down from heaven, and was incarnate by the Holy Spirit of the virgin Mary, and was made man; and was crucified also for us under Pontius Pilate; He suffered and was buried; and the third day He rose again, according to the Scriptures; and ascended into heaven, and sits on the right hand of the Father; and He shall come again, with glory, to judge the quick and the dead; whose kingdom shall have no end.

And I believe in the Holy Ghost, the Lord and Giver of Life; who proceeds from the Father [and the Son]; who with the Father and the Son together is worshiped and glorified; who spoke by the prophets.

And I believe in one holy catholic[2] and apostolic Church. I acknowledge one baptism for the remission of sins; and I look for the resurrection of the dead, and the life of the world to come. Amen.[3]

Our questions regarding orthodoxy tested for respondents' ability to accurately reflect the Nicene Creed, including things like the full divinity and full humanity of Jesus in one unified person, the Trinity, the sinlessness of Jesus, the death of Jesus on the cross for the penalty of sins, the resurrection of Jesus, the exclusivity of Jesus for salvation, and the reliability of the Bible.

Among this group in our survey, there is a very low belief in heaven (53%) and by far the lowest percentage of any group regarding belief in an actual hell (40%). They also disregard the reliability of the Bible as the standard for all matters of faith and practice.

When Things Start to Turn

This group is most religious during their late twenties. Beyond that age, practices such as prayer, worship attendance, fasting, and devotional reading decline significantly. Their incidence of leaving the church starts to accelerate during the 18–25 age range and continues through their early professional years. During this significant life station, the stress points they find particularly difficult include many social factors, such as struggling to fit in at church, having some bad experiences at church, a lack of people their age they connect with, life getting busy, having their main friends at work, and wanting to enjoy surplus income to travel and buy things.

Ideas and Attitudes

When analyzing the data, we only let the algorithm consider certain information about the individuals who participated in our study.

---

2. The word *catholic* here refers to the global or universal church and not merely to a single branch of the church such as Roman Catholicism.

3. Nicene Creed as hosted on https://www.ccel.org/creeds/nicene.creed.html.

One of the things we *didn't* allow the algorithm to access was the respondents' ethnicity or race. That factor clearly cast a long shadow over the results, however. Among the four evangelical subgroups that emerged, 98 percent of cultural Christians were white, 91 percent of dechurched mainstream evangelicals were white, 82 percent of exvangelicals[4] were white, and 0 percent of dechurched BIPOC[5] were white (we selected the name for this group because of this remarkable phenomenon). As a matter of fact, there may not be a single factor more influential in determining these subgroups, despite the fact that our algorithm was completely blind to ethnicity and race.

Tom is on the high end of both education and income for cultural Christians, but this group has the second-highest income and education of any evangelical subgroup, mainline, or Catholic. American institutions such as the government, economy, education system, media, and health care work well for them. The ladders of American society are accessible and useful as they navigate life and work to achieve their goals. They have strong upward mobility and little resentment toward American institutions.

As you might expect from a group that centers politically left, cultural Christians are moderately pro-choice, supported vaccine mandates for teachers, aren't aggressive on foreign military intervention, want increased gun control, and are concerned about climate change. However, it's important to appreciate the nuances our study revealed that go beyond the starkly divided partisan politics fostered by the national media.

While American institutions seem to be working well for this group, they also have great empathy for the rioters at the Capitol on January 6, 2021. A staggering 59 percent of cultural Christians agree that "the January 6 riot at the US Capitol was an effort by patriots to protect and restore our Christian nation." Even so, their Christian

4. Our third subgroup of dechurched evangelicals, of whom none are actively willing to return to an evangelical church.

5. BIPOC stands for Black, indigenous, and people of color.

nationalism score is only middle-of-the-road. Certainly the fact that this group is 98-percent white plays some role in these seemingly contradictory attitudes, but it's still difficult to reconcile such an ideological contrast.

Cultural Christians are not particularly racially sensitive. They had the highest percentage (54%) of members who believe "racial problems in the US are rare, isolated situations." However, cultural Christians report being quite turned off by the racial attitudes and actions of the previous generation.

Further complicating our understanding of this group, 55 percent of them agree with the statement, "The US military should support Vladimir Putin and Russia in their special military operation in Ukraine." We aren't sure if there is a populist, authoritarian, or intolerant strain here. However, if any of those factors were true, we would expect to see greater frustration with American institutions. The best we can figure is that cultural Christians have close relational ties with flyover and Rust Belt America while also caring less about the underdog on the world stage than others.

From a morality standpoint, this is a somewhat malleable group. They score comparatively low on their concern for ethical matters like discrimination, abortion, pornography, substance abuse, lying, stealing, and greed. However, they have an elevated prosperity gospel score, revealing that they might associate moral behaviors with material rewards of health and wealth. This dissonance hints at their lack of key gospel concepts, a factor that will become more evident as we go along.

Generation Gap

Tom's parents' refusal to listen frustrated Tom. It impacted both their family relationships and his personal willingness to return to an evangelical church. This core oversight on the part of Tom's parents parallels the feelings and experiences shared by other cultural Christians.

Figure 3.1. What Did Your Parent Do That Played a Role in Your Decision to Stop Attending?

Reasons Given	Cultural	BIPOC	Exvangelicals	Mainstream
All their emphasis on the culture war lost me over time	18%	20%	2%	7%
Lack of love, gentleness, kindness, and generosity	17%	17%	6%	9%
My faith was probably never my own and was mainly a borrowed faith from parents	17%	15%	6%	6%
Inability to listen	17%	23%	5%	5%
Racial attitudes or actions	16%	18%	5%	6%
My parents stopped going to church	15%	18%	6%	9%
My parents are one of the few things that actually causes me to want to return to church	15%	15%	2%	5%
Inability to engage with other viewpoints	15%	21%	5%	6%
Intolerance toward my views of gender	15%	18%	3%	3%
Strong support of Donald Trump and the political right	14%	14%	3%	5%
Their faith seemed more like it was about cultural and/or political power than salvation through Jesus	14%	13%	4%	6%
I just wanted Jesus without all the evangelical baggage	14%	19%	5%	6%
My parents stopped believing	14%	15%	3%	5%
Hypocritical attitudes or actions	14%	16%	6%	9%
Misogynistic attitudes or actions	14%	17%	3%	5%
Intolerance toward My views of politics	14%	15%	4%	5%
The last few years have shown some ugliness	13%	15%	4%	5%
Intolerance toward my views of sexuality	13%	15%	4%	4%
Strong support of Joe Biden and the political left	11%	21%	1%	4%
None of the above	4%	8%	6%	6%

This group feels deeply put off by their parents' commitment to the culture wars. An obvious common denominator between the cultural Christians and their culture-warrior parents is the role of "culture." The overlapping nomenclature points us to the deeper problem. If one generation bases their religious beliefs and practice on cultural issues, then when the next generation's culture departs from theirs, it forces a religious rift as well. Sadly, the dechurched feel that their parents don't offer them or others the basic kindness of listening to differing thoughts and opinions. Moreover, many report seeing little evidence of the fruit of the Spirit in their parents' lives.

Tom's story might have ended differently if his parents had cared to engage with him on his beliefs rather than simply spouting their own. It's not hard to imagine a scene in which they ask Tom about his thoughts and show loving respect for him, even if they don't sway in their own beliefs at all. Unfortunately, our data reveals that this type of open exchange has not been offered to many dechurched evangelicals. In response, the cultural Christians have some pointed advice for their parents: listen better, live out your faith, and be more charitable toward those with whom you disagree. We think that's good advice for any Christian, whether you have an adult child or not.

Why They Left and Why They Might Be Willing to Come Back

The reasons cultural Christians say they abandoned organized religion are social and experiential. When asked why they left the church, they responded with the reasons cited in figure 3.2.

Most people like Tom are casually dechurched. One can see the social challenges here to fit in, a lack of people their age, and some bad experiences in church. We can see that community and relationships are shifting to more online and at work. As for Tom, life gets busy and career success has opened leisure, travel, and other hobby activities. Church simply isn't a priority anymore. While there is certainly a bit of relational tension, the cultural Christians largely have not experienced significant church hurt. Simply put, the inertia of career, family, and other interests have sidelined church. These Christians were nominal to begin with in the depth of their knowledge of the basics. Christianity also no longer conferred to them any benefit in terms of career, social standing, or credibility. For some contexts, Christianity even began to take on negative connotations, and this likely contributed to the rate of dechurching among this group.

Figure 3.2. Reasons for Not Attending Church

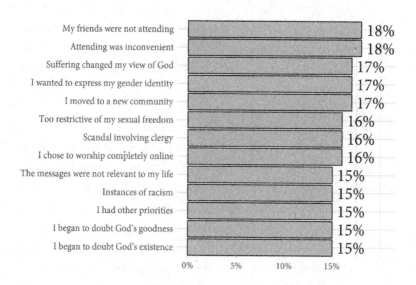

Reason	Percentage
My friends were not attending	18%
Attending was inconvenient	18%
Suffering changed my view of God	17%
I wanted to express my gender identity	17%
I moved to a new community	17%
Too restrictive of my sexual freedom	16%
Scandal involving clergy	16%
I chose to worship completely online	16%
The messages were not relevant to my life	15%
Instances of racism	15%
I had other priorities	15%
I began to doubt God's goodness	15%
I began to doubt God's existence	15%

There is tremendous good news in the middle of all this bad news. Half of the Toms out there are actively willing to return to an evangelical church. In fact, only 3 percent of them in our survey say they would *never* return. So what might cause them to return?

Many of the reasons cultural Christians gave are heavily social. There is an open door here, and the approach Rex took with Tom will likely prove fruitful. We will see throughout the different profiles in the book that some people need a nudge, others need a dinner table, and others need years of patient and prayerful, consistent movement into their lives. Tom and the cultural Christians largely need your dinner table. They probably won't oblige your nudge or invitation to return to church, as they need more relational connectivity than that. More than one person or household moving into Tom's life may be beneficial.

As good a friend and mentor as Rex is, his nudges over the phone probably won't win the day with Tom. People like Tom need consistent, real-world, and increasingly close friendship to be drawn back to church. The reality, though, is that over half are actively willing to go back *right now*, and almost none have totally ruled it out. This should give you tremendous hope to keep sincerely investing in people where they are at. Our hope is that you are encouraged that your efforts here are more likely to bear fruit than not if you have a mid-to-long view in mind.

Why Cultural Christians Can Be a Good Thing

In the past, the idea of a nominal or cultural Christian was often viewed negatively. It doesn't appear that many cultural Christians possess a saving faith. However, what if we saw things from a different perspective? In ancient Israel, the temple included various areas of increasing depth and connectivity to the faith. Running broadly with this idea, what if cultural Christians were to find their way into the metaphorical forecourt[6] of the church and then enter its inner court where deep saving faith can be found?

A robust space for people who are between belief and unbelief can be a good thing. Not everyone needs to belong before they believe and behave, but many do. The very makeup of the faith has

---

6. These ideas have been inspired by in-person conversations with James Eglinton and email correspondence with Tim Keller regarding their thoughts on some of the writings of Abraham Kuyper and Herman Bavinck.

certain rituals like baptism and the Lord's Supper that move us from the forecourt into the inner court once we publicly profess our faith. We don't want to see Christianity lose its forecourt where people belong even if they lack belief. That liminal space where people are still exploring, examining the faith, and in community with those with deep faith is important.

We invite you to think creatively about how your home and your local church might build a robust forecourt where folks like Tom might be able to reengage with the community and ideas of Christians. One historic confession used by Presbyterians around the world, the Westminster Shorter Catechism, refers to a concept called "the ordinary means of grace":

> **Q:** What are the outward and ordinary means whereby Christ communicates to us the benefits of redemption?
> **A:** The outward and ordinary means whereby Christ communicates to us the benefits of redemption are his ordinances, especially the word, sacraments, and prayer; all which are made effectual to the elect for salvation.[7]

Two-thirds of the ordinary means of grace—prayer and the Word—are fully available to anyone, regardless of where they are in their faith journey. We should not underestimate the value of having people be able to sit under such ordinary means as an extension of that forecourt. In other words, we want to see cultural Christians back in our churches because God frequently uses the ordinary means combined with Spirit-filled community as a means to draw people to himself.

---

7. Westminster Shorter Catechism, Question 88, Proclamation, PCA, September 8, 2016, http://proclamationpca.com/blog/2016/9/7/westminster-shorter-catechism-88.

How to Keep People from Becoming Cultural Christians

We have before us a tremendous opportunity in reengaging with all the Toms out there. These numbers quantify a literal example of that field Jesus described as being "white for harvest" (John 4:35). There could be 8 million Toms out there. You almost certainly have Toms in your relational circles.

Before they dechurched, cultural Christians needed authentic friendship and sincere community. They also needed to be ministered to and discipled earlier and with greater substance, especially in their teens and early twenties. Their doctrinal disparities reveal, at the very least, an absence of consistent, biblical discipleship. Religious behaviors don't make sense to them because they have substantial cracks in their spiritual foundations.

Many cultural Christians came from biblically and doctrinally shallow expressions of evangelicalism. But there is much life and vitality to be found in the historic creeds and confessions of our ancient faith. We want to see healthy local churches that clearly teach the Bible and catechize on the creeds and confessions.[8] We also want to see those churches have members who are well equipped to engage their contexts with relational wisdom.

We have a gospel that is true, good, and beautiful. Jesus is making all things new in the whole universe. His work of redemption accomplishes salvation for his entire church, but it also brings redemption as far as the curse is found. That means that everything that is broken, crooked, unjust, evil, or wicked will ultimately be made right, new, just, and whole.

---

8. Excellent creeds, confessions, and statements of faith can be drawn upon in a wide variety of traditions: the Thirty-Nine Articles, the Westminster Confession of Faith and the Larger and Shorter Catechisms, the 1689 Second London Baptist Confession, the Belgic Confession, the Heidelberg Catechism, the Canons of Dort, as well as more recent formulations like the New Hampshire Confession of Faith, the Baptist Faith and Message 2000, or the New City Catechism.

The gospel has more truth, goodness, and beauty wrapped up in it than a whole lifetime of intellectual studies, contemplative devotion, and active engagement can encapsulate. The cultural Christians would have been better served by this kind of expression of the faith.[9]

---

9. We will expand in greater detail on this theme in chapter 13, "Confessional and Missional."

Chapter 4

Dechurched Mainstream Evangelicals

GLASS SHATTERED IN EVERY DIRECTION, ICE CUBES SKITTERING across the travertine tile. Cold water saturated her socks. Hannah tried to keep her balance and not take a step.

Her nurse-sense told her she should probably eat something too. Having twin toddlers meant she often forgot to take care of her own basic needs. *This is why most women don't have babies in their late thirties*, she thought to herself.

Hannah had lived her whole life in Chapel Hill, North Carolina. Her mom was a researcher for GlaxoSmithKline, and her dad was an engineer for BioGen. She had the idyllic American childhood.

Cul-de-sac. White picket fence. Riding bikes. Pool parties. A *Jem* lunchbox. A Trapper Keeper binder.

Hannah was smart, like her parents. You would find *The Economist*, *The Atlantic*, *Popular Mechanics*, *Architectural Digest*, and *Time* on the coffee table.

Church was a huge part of their family's life; they were there every Sunday morning and every Wednesday night. This is what you did, after all, if you were Southern Baptist. Hannah asked Jesus into her heart at VBS when she was seven and was baptized soon afterward. She lived the full white evangelical subculture.

Adventures in Odyssey. Awana. Sword drills. See You at the Pole. True Love Waits. A purity ring from her dad. A mission trip to help build an orphanage and church in Mexico.

Her friend Amanda moved into the house across the street when Hannah was in middle school. Amanda's family also joined their church, and the two girls became fast friends. Amanda was a strong Christian too. Their senior year, they co-led a Bible study together for the freshmen girls.

Hannah went on to study nursing at UNC Chapel Hill while Amanda majored in chemical engineering at nearby NC State. They remained close throughout college, even though they were on different campuses. Amanda would come to UNC to go to InterVarsity with Hannah, and then they would go over to NC State to attend CRU meetings together.

When Hannah and Amanda graduated, they both got jobs in Research Triangle Park (a kind of Silicon Valley of the South) and rented an apartment together. Amanda worked for GlaxoSmithKline, and Hannah worked as a nurse at WakeMed. They both worked hard, were heavily involved with their large church, and did a lot of traveling in their time off.

Hannah met Jack at one of the young professionals events at their church. He was a tall, handsome, and successful commercial real estate broker. They had several mutual friends and discovered that their time at UNC even overlapped. They hit it off right away.

Durham Bulls. Ben Folds Five. Dave Matthews Band. Marriage and the honeymoon phase.

Neither of them could have predicted how difficult the next few years would be. Years of miscarriages, fertility doctors, and awkward procedures.

Thankfully, their church small group was there for them throughout the process. They faithfully prayed and walked with them through the ensuing roller coaster of hope and disappointment.

Still, the whole thing messed with Hannah's faith. She lay in bed at night with her mind racing. *What we're asking for is a good thing. I just want to have family dinners and love on the neighborhood kids and the ones at church. Why would God deny us that?*

In 2019 after three years of fertility treatments and several rounds of IVF, Hannah was finally pregnant—with twins! It was a high risk pregnancy due to her age and having multiples, so she quit her job and went on bed rest.

The twins were born prematurely in the middle of the initial COVID-19 lockdown, and they were at high risk for many complications. This both challenged and complicated Hannah's faith.

Little sleep. Postpartum depression. Social distancing. COVID-19 isolation.

Their community group had been wonderful, bringing meals for their first few weeks at home. They checked on them for the first few months of the pandemic, but everyone relationally drifted apart through the weirdness of the pandemic.

The whole thing felt like a storm had swept through and leveled their former existence. Every part of her life now was completely different from her life before pregnancy and COVID-19.

It was hard to believe they hadn't been to church since she went on bed rest three years ago. She had to admit it was much easier to do church online, not only initially for the babies' health but also because she didn't have to twist Jack's arm as much. He loved it because he could scroll Facebook and get some work done while church was happening. She liked it because they could have church while everyone was still eating frozen waffles in their pajamas.

Performing lifesaving medicine had been replaced with potty training, tantrums, and meal planning.

Sweeping the last few shards of glass into the dustpan, Hannah heard the little ones waking from their nap. She suddenly felt her own tears welling up. *This is not how I wanted to raise my kids,* she wept as a wave of guilt and grief washed over her. *Maybe I'll call Amanda tonight, if I'm not too tired.*

Understanding Dechurched Mainstream Evangelicals

Hannah is a mainstream evangelical who has dechurched. We know dozens of Hannahs.

This group looks radically different from the other four dechurched evangelical groups in numerous respects. Compared to the cultural Christians, they have a much higher orthodoxy score. It isn't surprising that when you drill down, they look most like evangelicals who *still go to church*. In fact, in almost every instance, evangelicals who are still churched and those who are dechurched from this group are virtually identical. Therefore, it will be enlightening for us to look closely at the points where they are different.

In our study, dechurched mainstream evangelicals (we'll call them DMEs) are slightly younger than churched mainstream evangelicals (CMEs), with an average age of 40 compared to age 50 among those still churched. CMEs are, on average, a little more educated and affluent. There are regional differences between the two groups in our survey, with DMEs being more evenly distributed across the country and CMEs more concentrated in the Southeast.[1]

CMEs are more politically conservative in our survey, with 45 percent identifying as Republican or strong Republican versus 31 percent for DMEs, who tend to lean more center-right. There are slightly more female DMEs (61%) than ones who are churched (56%).

---

1. Fifty-five percent of evangelicals who are still churched live in the Southeast, whereas only 29% of the DME group lives in the Southeast.

The center-right versus conservative difference holds true with policy as well (see fig. 4.1).

Interestingly, DMEs are more prone to thinking we are now in the end times (70% versus 58% for CMEs) in our survey. They also have a higher overall "prosperity gospel" score than those who are churched (59% versus 43%).

We discovered two more surprising and rather notable differences. The biggest surprise for this group is that they have a *more favorable* view of evangelicals (72%) than current churchgoing evangelicals do (61%). When we try to assess the reason for this difference, what is going on here is probably as simple as this—they haven't had negative experiences with church. Their dechurching is simply because a wide variety of circumstances have gotten them out of the habit. Anecdotally, we know several instances in which COVID-19, travel baseball, divorce, a new baby, or moving to another part of the city or a different state passively resulted in this type of dechurching. The second notable surprising difference was that DMEs had comparatively better mental health in our survey than those who still attend church. Pinpointing the reason for this dynamic is more difficult, but our sense is that there isn't much friction in the lives of DMEs. They have good educations, good incomes, and a high marital rate, and they are relatively young and haven't had many negative experiences in the church. Therefore, it makes sense that their older still-churched evangelical peers would be experiencing worse mental health scores on things like anxiety, depression, loneliness, and suicidal thoughts.

As introduced in chapter 3, DMEs hold to the tenets of the Nicene Creed. They held the highest scores on orthodox views and had a very high view of Jesus and the Bible. DMEs almost exclusively believe Jesus is the Son of God (98% versus 88% for CMEs), and most of them would tell you the Bible is the literal Word of God (59% versus 56% for CMEs).

Figure 4.1. Issue Positions of Still Churched and Dechurched Evangelicals

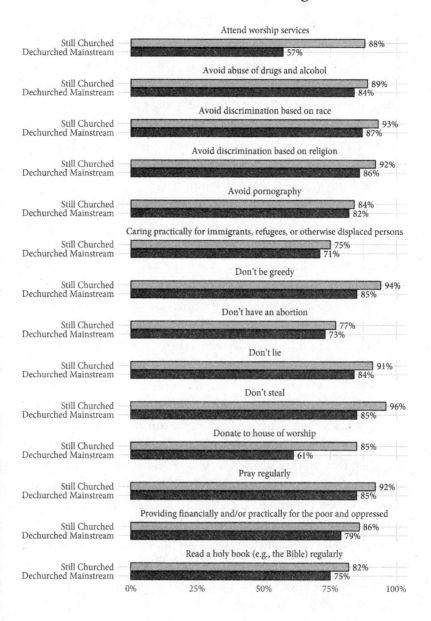

Attend worship services
Still Churched 88%
Dechurched Mainstream 57%

Avoid abuse of drugs and alcohol
Still Churched 89%
Dechurched Mainstream 84%

Avoid discrimination based on race
Still Churched 93%
Dechurched Mainstream 87%

Avoid discrimination based on religion
Still Churched 92%
Dechurched Mainstream 86%

Avoid pornography
Still Churched 84%
Dechurched Mainstream 82%

Caring practically for immigrants, refugees, or otherwise displaced persons
Still Churched 75%
Dechurched Mainstream 71%

Don't be greedy
Still Churched 94%
Dechurched Mainstream 85%

Don't have an abortion
Still Churched 77%
Dechurched Mainstream 73%

Don't lie
Still Churched 91%
Dechurched Mainstream 84%

Don't steal
Still Churched 96%
Dechurched Mainstream 85%

Donate to house of worship
Still Churched 85%
Dechurched Mainstream 61%

Pray regularly
Still Churched 92%
Dechurched Mainstream 85%

Providing financially and/or practically for the poor and oppressed
Still Churched 86%
Dechurched Mainstream 79%

Read a holy book (e.g., the Bible) regularly
Still Churched 82%
Dechurched Mainstream 75%

0%   25%   50%   75%   100%

Dechurched Mainstream
Evangelicals Overview

The average dechurched mainstream evangelical in our survey is 40 years old and most likely dropped out of church in the vicinity of 2020, during the COVID-19 pandemic. This subgroup is predominantly female (61%) and has a higher average income, education, and rate of marriage than the other four subgroups.

According to our study, 20 percent of DMEs now identify as Catholic and 21 percent as "Other Christian." As we saw reflected in Hannah's story, this group has a relatively high rate of involvement in both youth groups and campus ministry.

DMEs, as we saw earlier, trend center-right in their political affiliation and policy. They are not keen on supporting the January 6 riot (34%) or Russia's war on Ukraine (27%). They feel that US institutions are serving them well, with the highest confidence levels of all five groups in marriage (63%) and police (54%). Alternatively in our survey, they do not have high confidence in newspapers (30%), cable news (30%), big tech (29%), Congress (28%), or Wall Street (25%). DMEs spend less time on social media than any group except for the exvangelicals.

Why Did They Stop Going to Church?

While it's easy to understand how Hannah transitioned from COVID-19 lockdowns to livestream church to dechurching altogether, that process was not inevitable, either for her or the rest of the DMEs. With such high levels of orthodoxy (and, we would hope, accompanying faith), it feels like it wouldn't take much to get most of these folks back in church. Such hopeful numbers raise the question, why exactly did this group get stuck on the speed bump of COVID-19?

The biggest reasons why mainstream evangelicals dechurched in our survey can be seen in figure 4.2.

Figure 4.2. Reasons for Leaving Church

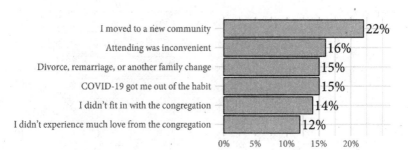

When we look at all the data, it seems like this group primarily either moved or got out of the habit of going to church. Maybe there is something we can point to like COVID-19, or maybe the reasons are more nebulous and difficult to pinpoint. Either way, this group does not hold church in contempt, and that is good news.

What we can't yet measure is what will happen to these numbers if DMEs remain out of church for several more years. Will they end up looking like some of the other groups, becoming less orthodox, having fewer spiritual disciplines, and experiencing greater relational drift? Our hunch is that a lack of community and gathered corporate worship may begin to erode their beliefs and practices over time.

The most important thing to know about dechurched mainstream evangelicals is that 100 percent of those in our study are *actively* willing to return to an evangelical church. This fact gives us tremendous hope. That is potentially 2.2 million people who say they would return to church right now. Here's what they told us would bring them back.

Four Avenues of Return

According to our study, the top reasons the dechurched would return to an evangelical church can be seen in figure 4.3.

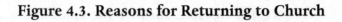

Figure 4.3. Reasons for Returning to Church

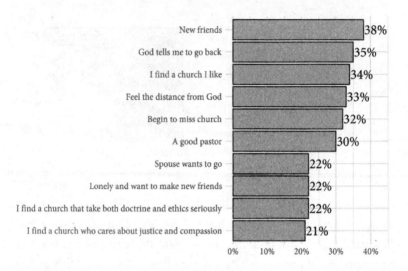

Within these responses, we can see four possible on-ramps[2] that might lead this group back to an evangelical church:

- There is a *social* on-ramp of experiencing loneliness, making new friends, or having a spouse who wants to go.
- There is the *church* on-ramp of missing church or finding a good church or pastor.
- There is the *God* on-ramp of hearing from God or lamenting distance from him.
- There is the *philosophy of ministry* on-ramp of finding a church that takes doctrine and ethics seriously or one that prioritizes justice and compassion for the vulnerable.

With these avenues in mind, you can see why DMEs could benefit from a good friend like Amanda to invite them to church,

---

2. We are grateful to our friend Jeremy Schurke for introducing us to the analogy of an off-ramp regarding dechurching. That off-ramp analogy was helpful to us here to formulate the idea of an on-ramp.

small group, or Bible study. They need people to pray for them, that the Holy Spirit would move in their hearts. And they need churches that are doing more tangible good in their communities, especially for those who need it most. Hannah thought of calling Amanda that night if she had the energy. How would the story be different if Amanda called Hannah?

Our hunch is that if Amanda picked up the phone to reconnect with Hannah, she might find her old friend more than happy to go to church with her. It is reasonable that Amanda could help Hannah think creatively and find ways to overcome the issues of childcare, health concerns, and other obstacles that feel so impossible right now.

As we noted in chapter 3, we think about the spectrum of where people are at in terms of just needing a nudge, being around your dinner table, or requiring years of ongoing close friendship. Our sense is that DMEs are mainly people who just need a few nudges to come back to church. We have had a number of people in our own lives who have started coming back to church with just a single invitation.

If you see yourself in Hannah's story, would you prayerfully consider finding a good church again? Can I be the first person to nudge you right now to make going back to church a priority again? Jesus wants us to not just love him but also love the family for which he gave up his whole life.

Perhaps you identified with Amanda's role in this story. If so, would you prayerfully go through your contacts, reconnect with two or three Hannahs, and see what God does in those conversations?

More than anything, dechurched mainstream evangelicals need a friend to reach out. They clearly know the gospel and are not Christians in name only. They just lack someone who cares enough to check in, see how they're doing, and extend a personal invitation. Remember that 100 percent of Hannahs are willing to come back to church today. Reaching out to DMEs does not pose a significant relational risk. Hannah *wants* Amanda to call her.

Ministry leaders in local churches will find a lot to consider here. Does your church have a membership process, and do you have ways to know if some of your members have gone missing?[3] Are you willing to call Hannah up and see how you can help make it easier for her and her family to return to church? If you still have a livestream, have you considered maybe just publishing video later in the week and encouraging the folks only worshiping online to return? Our church decided to turn off our livestream when the complexities of COVID-19 were dying down, and it was quite helpful in regathering the church in corporate worship.[4]

One of the saddest realities when people dechurch is that they aren't just losing the benefit of being in community with other people; those other people are losing the benefit of being in community with the dechurched person. The Christian faith is communal. When we cut ourselves off from embodied corporate worship, we deprive ourselves of the Lord's Supper, congregational worship, and community. When you look at all the fifty-nine "one another's" in the New Testament, the overwhelming majority of them require physical presence. We know the church will always have people who are sick, shut-in, and have other factors that actually preclude the possibility of corporate worship (and we must care for these people too), but Hannah and the DMEs are largely not that group.

Whether you see yourself in Hannah, have people like her in your life, or have responsibilities in your local church or ministry, it is always good for us to check in on the people in our lives. We hope you will take some time to reach out to a friend, catch up, pray, and maybe go to church together again.

Chapter 5

Exvangelicals

THANKSGIVING TRAFFIC PILING UP ON I-95, AND THE LINE AT HER gas station register is slammed.

Tammy is bone tired.

She is looking forward to getting home to her Cup O' Noodles and channel surfing to self-medicate another holiday alone.

Tammy grew up a latchkey kid under two blue-collar hard-working parents, Robert, a white Jacksonville native, and her part Jamaican part Puerto Rican mom, Destiny.

Fifty-four was not kind to Tammy. She makes only a little more than minimum wage even though she has always worked hard. Her underresourced schools growing up didn't do her any favors, and she never could find the ladders to help break the generational cycles of poverty.

Tammy became a Christian in elementary school, and she still prays and reads her Bible as an adult, even though she's done with church. She grew up in a somewhat charismatic nondenominational church. It wasn't even a question of whether they were going. The whole family was there every Sunday morning and Sunday night.

Growing up Tammy had hidden the fact that her grandma was Black. Racial tensions were high in that area, and Black students and white students often fought at her high school. She looked white enough that none of the girls ever questioned her race. It would have been a lot harder for her to fit in with her church friends if they saw her as being anything but white.

Her attitudes about her heritage changed over the years, though. She saw herself drifting from the people she had always called church family.

She saw Trayvon Martin, Eric Garner, Philando Castile, Ahmaud Arbery, Breonna Taylor, and George Floyd.

Tammy no longer had shame around the Afro-Caribbean and Puerto Rican part of her heritage.

Some of the stuff her old church friends were posting online was shocking, maddening, and really disheartening. After January 6, she just deleted social media altogether.

Tammy wasn't superpolitical, but she voted in the big elections. She felt alienated by both political parties but especially abandoned by the Republican party. It wasn't even recognizable anymore to her.

Thanksgiving had her thinking about her daughter Lily.

Her marriage started out okay. She met Wade in youth group, and they got married after high school graduation. Their life together mirrored her parents, grinding several low-wage jobs to get by.

Wade eventually got his welding certification. He got a good job at the port, Lily was born, and things were sweet for a while. They found a large Southern Baptist Church near their downtown apartment. They missed their old church family, but this one had an abundance of opportunities for Lily, with an attached preschool and a mother's day out program.

Everything was going well—until it didn't.

The economy turned. Wade got laid off. Then there was the sub-prime mortgage collapse. They foreclosed.

Wade self-medicated with drugs and got physical with her.

Lord, please help us, Tammy had prayed. *Help me know how to go forward. Please, God, help me protect my child.*

She tried asking their church if they could help them out. They told her the benevolence fund only provided one month of rent or mortgage payment per needy family. Of course, that wouldn't help their situation now.

When she asked the pastor about marriage counseling and help for Wade's drinking, he explained that he didn't recommend either twelve-step recovery or "psychology," since he believed both were rooted in unbiblical teaching. They said she didn't have enough reason for a divorce.

Her anger and frustration grew. Finally, she packed up and moved her and Lily to a women's shelter even though she knew their church wouldn't be happy.

Food stamps. Medicaid. Shared bathroom.

Tammy and Lily eventually got a tiny apartment in a housing project.

A year passed, and her daughter was still doing poorly at school. Tammy knew there must be more bothering her than she let on. She kept gently prodding her to open up until, finally, she was able to get the awful truth out of her little girl's shattered heart. In the summer of 2009, she had gone to a Christian camp with their church youth group. At that camp, one of their own church staff members had sexually assaulted her.

Tammy's world seemed to close in on her. She already had friction with the leadership of the church over her divorce, but this was inexcusable. The more she thought about it, the more furious she got. After church the following Sunday, she cornered and confronted the senior pastor. He promised her that he would personally handle the situation. The staff member was placed on an administrative leave of absence.

Weeks and months passed, and Lily's perpetrator was still on the payroll. Nobody from the church had even talked to her or Lily about the incident. Tammy finally called the police. From them she learned that, even though a pastor is what they call a "mandatory reporter" of sexual crimes against minors, they never filed a police report.

Tammy was done.

Done!

She never went back to church after that betrayal. The pain of it shredded her spirit. On top of the sexual abuse and the subsequent coverup, the treatment they received from fellow church members just rubbed salt in their wounds. Many of her friends in the church turned on her and lied about her and Lily. It got so bad that Lily refused to testify on record about her sexual abuse, so her case was never prosecuted.

Eight years later, Tammy still believes in Jesus, still reads her Bible and prays faithfully, but she can't bring herself to go back to church.

Lily grew up, moved out, and has her own issues now. She made some choices that Tammy isn't proud of. They both deal with a wide variety of problems as a result of these experiences. Anxiety, depression, distrust, and sometimes even suicidal thoughts have left their mark on every aspect of their lives.

Tammy turned the TV off and turned in for the night.

When the house is quiet and the TV is off, loneliness is her only companion.

Understanding Exvangelicals

Tammy is a member of the group we will refer to as exvangelicals. People who fit this profile comprise 17 percent of dechurched evangelicals in our survey. There may be more than 2 million adult Americans who, like Tammy, have permanently, purposefully exited evangelicalism. There isn't one exvangelical in our survey who is

actively willing to return to an evangelical church. Exvangelicals are
probably the most likely profile people picture in their minds when
they think about dechurching. Unlike other groups that are popu-
lated more by people who have casually dechurched, exvangelicals
are *dechurched casualties.*

It's important to note that we are using the term *exvangelical* in
a way that might be different from some online discourse you've
encountered. *Exvangelical*, as used in the current public forum, can
apply to a range of possibilities, from still-serious Christians who
merely eschew evangelical expressions of Christianity to those who
have left their former faith behind altogether.

Many of the self-described exvangelicals who feature prominently in online communities don't resemble Tammy much at all.
They are often well-spoken, well-educated, and media savvy. In our
research, however, we spoke to a number of thought leaders in these
exvangelical communities and learned that their inboxes are full
of messages from struggling, divorced, and single moms who are
wrestling with their faith. Therefore, please keep in mind that we
aren't trying to commandeer or redefine the term. Rather, we want
to help flesh out aspects of this community that you might not otherwise encounter or envision.

Demographics

According to our study, exvangelicals are 82 percent white,
13 percent Black, and 2 percent Hispanic. Most remarkably, they are
65 percent female and only 35 percent male. Their average age right
now is 54 years old (1969 birth year), and on average they dechurched
twenty years ago (2003).

As we can see from Tammy's story, exvangelicals have the lowest
income and education of all the groups we surveyed. They are also
more politically independent than the other groups, but this belief
diverges a bit in practice. Their political affiliation is center-left,
but their policy is a bit more moderate on issues such as abortion,

COVID-19, foreign policy, gun control, global warming, same-sex marriage, and more. Exvangelicals are the most critical of socialism, democratic socialism, Marxism, and communism. They are not a partisan group, having by far the largest percentage of independents (55%). Like Tammy, they don't care for either political party and were the most politically disinterested group of the five in this book. It seems clear from the data that both political parties have failed at addressing their core concerns.

Exvangelicals have relatively average representation across the country and are similar to the mainstream evangelical group in regard to regionality. They have the lowest rate of marriage of any group, at 54 percent. Conversely, they have the highest rates of singleness (20%), divorce (17%), and widowhood (10%). The majority (62%) of this group does not work full-time. They have the largest retired population (33%) and homemakers (9%). They are the most well-rooted (86% made no move in the last year), with their only moves usually occurring within the same city. The older age, percentage of retirees and homemakers, divorce and singleness rates, low rate of employment, and gender imbalance help us understand some of the significant demographic differences regarding income, education, and disenfranchisement.

Information Diet, Attitudes, and Relational Dynamics

Exvangelicals in our survey primarily trust broadcast news (23%), CNN (20%), and Fox News (16%). Relative to the other respondents, they are below average in being informed on current events and issues.

Their *overall* mental health is the second highest of all the other groups; however, their anxiety, depression, and loneliness are quite high. Even more troubling, this group ranks highest in suicidal thoughts. When we asked exvangelicals, "How would you score your well-being on suicidal thoughts? (Scale ranging from 0 to 100 with 0 being very negative and unhealthy and 100 being very positive and healthy)," their answer averaged only 16 out of 100. This score was so heartbreaking, I (Mike) cried the first time I saw it.

Exvangelicals in our survey spend the least amount of time on social media by far. When they do so, it is primarily on Facebook (11 hours per week) and YouTube (9 hours per week). They had the lowest approval rating for both Donald Trump (36%) and Joe Biden (35%).[1]

This subgroup looks to friends (42%), internet searches (32%), and most of all themselves (60%) for counsel. Their "looking to myself for answers on life's issues" is by far the highest of all the other dechurched evangelical groups. This figure is three times that of the cultural Christians (21%) and twice that of the dechurched BIPOCs (32%). This trend makes us even more concerned for the well-being of this group. Isolation and loneliness are serious concerns to address when ministering to exvangelicals. Tammy is a good example of someone who is in almost constant contact with people all day yet is moving through life alone.

Doctrine, Beliefs, and Church Involvement

Even though the exvangelicals in our survey are actively unwilling to return to an evangelical church, they are the second most orthodox subgroup. Overall they affirmed between 70 percent of key doctrinal questions concerning the Trinity, the divinity/humanity of Jesus, his sinlessness, atonement, resurrection, and exclusivity, and the reliability of the Bible. A surprising 97 percent of them still believe that "Jesus is the Son of God." Furthermore, a second-highest score of 44 percent agree that the Bible is the literal Word of God, and 47 percent believe that the Bible is at least divinely inspired, if not to be taken completely literally. Ninety-three percent of them still believe in heaven, and 88 percent believe in hell. Collectively,

---

1. They were also deeply distrustful of Vladimir Putin (16% approval) and Russia's war on Ukraine (12% approval), perhaps showing empathy for the underdog and a distrust of those in power.

exvangelicals have the second-highest percentage of people who still self-identify as Christians, at 72 percent.

From every measurable perspective, it seems like *most* exvangelicals in our survey are still Christians. Their religious beliefs and behaviors aren't much different from evangelicals who still attend church. The main difference is that their religious *belonging* has shifted. Although no longer part of an evangelical church, 32 percent still describe themselves as Protestant. Others have switched affiliation, with 20 percent of them self-identifying as "Other Christian," and 19 percent as Catholic.

Like Tammy, the average exvangelical in our survey is 54 years old, but they dechurched at an average age of 34. This group had the second-lowest level of involvement in youth groups (27%) and the absolute lowest level of participation in church-based college and campus ministry (4–6%). Exvangelicals deeply dislike the ongoing evangelical culture wars. They have tried fewer churches than all the other groups, averaging attendance at only 3.7 churches over the course of their lifetimes.

Exvangelicals' highest belief in the existence of God coincided with their highest level of religious involvement; their belief has fallen off a little bit since. At that peak, they also scored near the same levels as mainstream evangelicals on religious behaviors such as prayer, worship attendance, fasting, and devotional reading. Those numbers have dropped off significantly now, but they are still above cultural Christians and BIPOC. Exvangelicals were slightly below average on the Christian nationalism score but were extremely put off by the events of January 6, 2021, with only 16 percent affirming the riots at the US Capitol.

Institutional Breakdown

A recurring theme that featured prominently in our data was the fact that American institutions are not working well for exvangelicals in our survey. Aside from marriage (49%), police (41%), and democracy (37%), not a single US institution had more than 33 percent confidence of this group. Some institutions in which exvangelicals have particularly low confidence are the public education system (27%), criminal justice system (25%), big technology companies (22%), US Congress (20%), newspapers (18%), and Wall Street (16%).

Not only are these secular institutions deeply failing them, but religious ones have let them down as well. Their confidence levels in most church groups hovered around the one-quarter mark, with nondenominational churches at 28 percent, Black Protestants at 26 percent, evangelicals at 25 percent, mainline Protestants at 24 percent, and Catholics at a low of 21 percent.

As previously mentioned, there are statistically proven paths to success in America, including graduating high school, working full-time, and marrying before having children.[2] Ninety-seven percent of millennials who follow this "success sequence" live above the poverty line. Tammy certainly didn't receive the education she needed. The macroeconomic headwinds of the subprime mortgage collapse fell disproportionately hard on her and Wade. Those effects were so catastrophic that it brought out the worst in Wade's character. Who is to say that those character weaknesses might not have otherwise surfaced if they'd had better relational and monetary safety nets? As with many exvangelicals, Tammy was failed by many American institutions. She didn't do anything to cause the tremendous difficulties she experienced. Many exvangelicals find themselves in a similar state of affairs. For them, at least, America is not necessarily a meritocracy.

This study reveals that exvangelicals have fallen through the cracks, not only in American society, but within evangelicalism too. They left their churches because they already felt left behind there relationally, socially, politically, and in many other ways. We will

---

2. W. Bradford Wilcox and Wendy Wang, "The Power of the Success Sequence," American Enterprise Institute, May 26, 2022, https://www.aei.org/research-products/report/the -power-of-the-success-sequence.

discuss the implications of this religious exile in more depth in chapter 14, "Embracing Exile." First, let's see what this group says about why they left.

Why They Left

Exvangelicals had *some* things in common with other dechurched evangelical groups, with similar social reasons and inconvenience for leaving. However, we can see more frequent and deeper pain in their answers. For example, only exvangelicals had these two choices in their top six:

> I didn't experience much love within the congregation. (18%)
> Negative experiences you personally had in an evangelical
>   church. (15%)

Exvangelicals in our survey scored 74 percent higher on having experienced a lack of love from their congregations than the other four groups *combined*. On top of that, they scored twice as high as any other group on "negative experiences you personally had in an evangelical church." To imagine the frustration and righteous anger of knowing that your daughter has been sexually assaulted and nothing will ever be done about it is to start to understand the perspective of some exvangelicals. If this or other religious abuses or abandonment happened to your family, wouldn't you become a church casualty too?

Exvangelicals also struggle with the political partisanship found in many evangelical churches today. They represent millions of theologically orthodox Christians who lean independent to center-left in their political identity and policies. Regardless of tradition, churches that espouse heavy, right-leaning politics will be difficult places for exvangelicals to feel at home. They are also likely to experience tension in deeply progressive congregations, particularly where a departure from historic orthodoxy has taken place.

Figure 5.1 shows the top reasons exvangelicals in our survey say they decided to dechurch.

Figure 5.1. Reasons for Not Attending Church

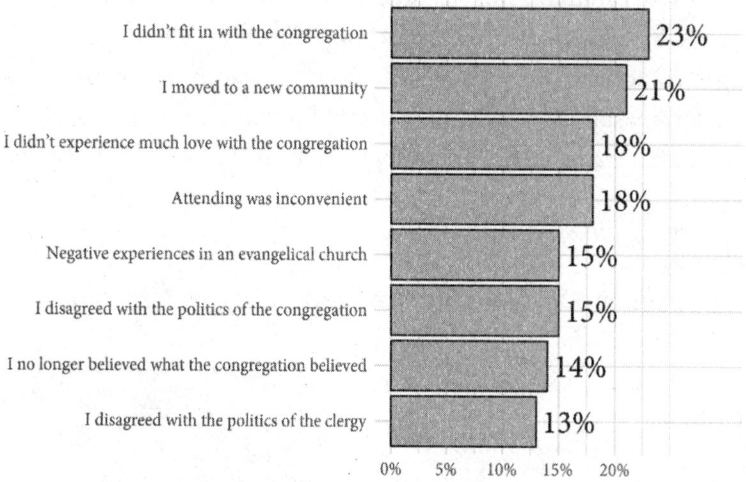

Reason	Percentage
I didn't fit in with the congregation	23%
I moved to a new community	21%
I didn't experience much love with the congregation	18%
Attending was inconvenient	18%
Negative experiences in an evangelical church	15%
I disagreed with the politics of the congregation	15%
I no longer believed what the congregation believed	14%
I disagreed with the politics of the clergy	13%

Dechurching starts to accelerate for this group in their teens and twenties. As with dechurched mainstream evangelicals, one item that brightly stands out in their twenties is that "life got really busy and I had other priorities" (7%). Also similar is that a fair amount of dechurching happens around the empty-nest transition. This group has no qualms about leaving the traditions in which they were raised. Rather, they report that their parents' faith hardly played any role in their decision to dechurch.

Why They Would Be Willing to Return to an Evangelical Church

The heartbreaking truth is that 0 percent of exvangelicals in our survey are actively willing to return to an evangelical church. Zero percent! They are done.

The good news is that there are plenty of gospel-preaching churches that aren't in the evangelical tradition. We have many pastor friends deeply committed to the gospel in Black Protestant and mainline traditions. We don't think it is ideal for people to be out of fellowship with Christ's body, and we would like to see these individuals loved, cared for, and pastored.

Oddly enough, despite their claims of being completely unwilling to come back to an evangelical church, exvangelicals still offered us a few reasons why they might be willing to come back to a different church tradition if some things changed. These reasons can be seen in figure 5.2.

Figure 5.2. Reasons for Returning to Church

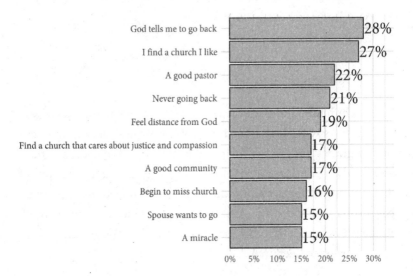

What Can We Do?

For those who care to notice, the pain felt by our exvangelical brothers and sisters is palpable. Despite their best efforts, institutions of all kinds have failed them. The supposedly normal avenues to security and safe community proved to be dead ends. If that isn't your experience, our goal is to help you increase your empathy for their trauma. The attitude with which you engage with exvangelicals is essential to the mission. Winning their trust will require humility, active listening, calmness, and a posture of curiosity.

When we dial in the things they've told us, the picture is clear: exvangelicals need a nonpartisan church community that is consistent in their ethics. They need local churches that don't just contain some healthy people but are actually healthy as an institution. They need church environments that value mental health. They need real understanding, empathy, and care from pastors and laypeople alike. They need clergy who know the limits of their areas of expertise and at what point other professionals need to be called in. If we think about these characteristics that would be helpful for exvangelicals, are these not qualities that would be good in any and every local church?

Exvangelicals need people who will commit to establishing authentic, long-term relationships with them even before there is enough substance to invite them to church events. They need a church that is consistent in word and deed. Given the empirical gap in education and income, they need Christians who set aside societal class distinctions like Jesus did.

While Tammy's story is on the more painful end of the exvangelical spectrum, it helps us understand exvangelicals' mindsets and needs. She just wants someone to genuinely look her in the eye and hear her out. Tammy needs validation that the things she has seen are not the way they should be. She needs people in her life who will treat her with dignity as a fellow human who bears the image of God. She needs church leaders who love vulnerable people enough to have proactively placed safeguards in place or at a minimum to rapidly take ownership, become educated, and institute organizational change to prevent such future excruciating circumstances.

Even when we understand all these factors, it will still be difficult to minister to exvangelicals, especially in traditional established church environments. This challenge should not preclude, hinder, or temper our efforts to love and care well. However, we must avoid pride and overconfidence in our abilities. Sometimes the Lord asks us to simply show up and love our neighbor as ourselves. Go and do likewise.

Chapter 6

Dechurched BIPOC

THE FOG CONDENSED INTO DRIZZLE AS JEREMIAH RAN. THE FALL IN Atlanta *can* be good running weather, but that was not the case tonight. He missed going to the gym with Liz that evening because one of his transplant patients received the call they had been waiting on for almost a year.

The mist collected on his close-shaved head, chilling him quickly and stinging his ears. He wished he could pull up the hood on his Notre Dame sweatshirt. *Maybe I could get away with it just this once,* he thought. Just as quickly, he heard his mom's voice lecturing him every time he left the Army base as a teenager. *If a police officer tells you to do something, you obey immediately. Keep your hands out of your pockets. Keep that hood off your head.*

It just wasn't worth it. He'd already had the cops called on him twice in as many years by nervous white neighbors in their elite gated neighborhood. It didn't matter that he and Liz had lived there for almost sixteen years or that he was the top cardiothoracic surgeon at Emory University Hospital. All it took was one new person in the neighborhood who hadn't met him yet to have yet another set of guns pulled on him.

Jeremiah hadn't thought about those years at Fort Benning in a long time, but he thought about his dad every single day. Glenroy was a stoic sergeant major in the Army and was tough as nails.

Jeremiah's mom, Mavis, was gentle, kind, and nurturing, but she was also no pushover. She was very structured and had high expectations for her only child. It helped that his mom was relentlessly supportive and involved in his schoolwork. Her ancestors suffered picking cotton in Georgia plantations.

Glenroy and Mavis were an odd couple in some regards. Glenroy was a second generation Jamaican American and an outspoken Republican. Mavis was a descendant of American slaves and a Democrat. Glenroy got his degree from Penn State, and Mavis went to Spelman. They only met because of the little AME church near the Army base, but when their paths finally crossed, they were joined for life. Mavis liked that Glenroy was driven, reliable, and a man of his word. Glenroy liked Mavis because she was smart, motivated, and reasonable.

Nothing Jeremiah did was good enough to satisfy his dad, but he tried anyway. As a result, Jeremiah was valedictorian of his high school class and earned a full ride to Notre Dame, a top premed school.

Jeremiah's faith was never what you would call strong. He went to church with his parents because that was the expectation. It was never quite clear whether the source of his faith was personal or simply compliance with his parents' wishes. Only time would tell if his faith was a borrowed one or a faith that would become fully his own.

Before long, Jeremiah started dating a white girl from the nondenominational church. Alice was from Birmingham, Alabama. Jeremiah really liked her and enjoyed getting to meet her parents when they came up to campus for a visit. He thought the meet-and-greet was going well until he mentioned that he would like to visit them during the Christmas break in Birmingham.

Alice acted reluctant and somewhat evasive after his comment.

Later, Jeremiah pressed her as to why she didn't seem to like the idea. Deeply embarrassed, she confessed that her grandmother didn't approve of interracial relationships, so the family had kept it a secret that she was dating a Black man. Jeremiah was stunned. He was incredulous that she wouldn't stick up for him with her family. He hadn't had a racial or relational experience like this one before, it stung hard, and naturally he ended the relationship.

Not long after, Jeremiah was driving back to South Bend and got pulled over. The officer had his hand on his holstered gun as he approached the driver's side window. Before asking for his license or registration, the cop instructed him to get out of the car slowly and put his hands on the hood. Jeremiah was a little scared but tried to keep his composure. He was frisked, cuffed, asked a bunch of questions about where he was going and what he had been doing. The officer then asked for permission to search the vehicle and threw him in the back of the squad car. After what seemed like an hour, the officer pulled him out, uncuffed him, and said he was free to go. Jeremiah asked what he had done wrong, and the officer simply said, "You fit a profile." Although he had heard secondhand about other African Americans' challenges with police, it affected him when it happened to him. From that moment on, Jeremiah felt tightness in his chest every time he saw flashing blue police lights.

By this time, Jeremiah was eager to get out of Indiana. Just as he had done in high school, he put his head down and treated school like it was his job. He shifted into military mode, becoming more regimented and disciplined. Soon he had cranked out his premed degree, graduating magna cum laude.

He went on to Columbia for medical school on the Army scholarship program. Mavis hoped he might connect more with his roots and the rich history in neighboring Harlem, but he never quite availed himself to plumb the depths of Harlem's culture and heritage. To placate her, they would go to Abyssinian Baptist when she came to visit.

He would graduate and move on to do his residency in Boston at Beth Israel Deaconess Medical Center and trained under a talented Black surgeon who encouraged him to pursue cardiothoracics as his specialty.

Those years were tiring and stressful. He was practicing actual medicine with real-world risks. He stopped going to church altogether except when his mom came to town.

Since his faith didn't seem to help him, and he never felt like the messages were relevant to his life, he didn't miss it. He also didn't have the mental energy to deal with the same cringey comments from his old nondenominational church at Notre Dame: "You are so articulate," or "I don't see race," or his personal favorite, white people's unsolicited stories about their one Black friend. Those interactions alone weren't the fatal blow to his church experience, but along with everything else he had going on, he found himself wondering, *Why am I going to church again?*

Jeremiah satisfied his obligation to the Army in San Antonio at Brooke Army Medical Center. There he met Liz, a razor-sharp nurse who actually reminded him of his Mom—smart, pretty, clear-eyed, and driven. Liz was not a Christian, but she wasn't opposed to it either. When it came to faith, Liz wasn't anything in particular. She existed in that liminal space between belief and unbelief. This didn't bother Jeremiah, as that description wasn't much different from his own religious malaise. He was just happy Liz's grandparents didn't object to their white granddaughter marrying a Black man.

Lots of changes happened quickly after they married. They were thrilled when Liz got pregnant just four months after the wedding. Glenroy had recently retired from the Army, and Jeremiah's parents settled in Atlanta since the city was special to Mavis from her time at Spelman. Jeremiah and Liz both wanted to keep practicing medicine but knew they would need help with the baby, so they took jobs at Emory University Hospital. Not long after their move, they welcomed little baby Adelaide to the family.

Atlanta worked well for their family on many levels. Both Jeremiah and Liz came to be well-loved and respected at Emory, establishing strong reputations among their peers and superiors. Glenroy and Mavis were proud, doting grandparents. Mavis was especially happy to have a helping role again and loved getting to spend so much time with her granddaughter, especially during those formative years.

Despite being in Atlanta, their world was almost totally white. They found a beautiful house in one of Atlanta's elite neighborhoods near top shelf private schools. Their daughter was always one of the only children of color in class. Their jobs provided every material thing they had ever wanted. Jeremiah knew he was incredibly privileged. Whether at work, at home, or socially, his race wasn't a big factor in his life at all except when he had the cops called on him.

Outwardly, people experienced Jeremiah as a confident and successful surgeon, but inwardly, he still battled insecurity trying to earn his dad's affection. He masked the pain by self-medicating through work, exercise, and bourbon.

Jeremiah was determined not to be his dad, so he strove to have a close relationship with Adelaide. Their investments in her were paying off, and she'd be going off to college.

He finished his run, cleared his head, and prepared himself psychologically for another family meal.

It wasn't a family meal if there wasn't talk about politics and religion. Mavis and Glenroy had their usual back and forth, but Jeremiah was politically agnostic. He didn't want to be taxed into oblivion, but he didn't want to be harassed by police either. He had more in common with Susan Rice, Colin Powell, or Ben Carson than he did with Jerry Rice, Colin Kaepernick, or Ben Wallace. At the end of the day, Mavis was just grateful he didn't vote for Trump like his dad did.

Mavis kept pressing him to lean into his heritage and to his former faith. He was respectful in those conversations, but they were uncomfortable because while he still believed in God, church wasn't working for him and hadn't for a long time. Jeremiah could tell there was a sadness in his mom about where he was with Jesus, and he felt bad about that. Even so, he wasn't going to go through the motions to make his mom feel better.

The tryptophan induced post-Thanksgiving sleepiness was running its course, and Jeremiah called it early for the night.

Understanding Dechurched BIPOC

BIPOC (pronounced "bye-pock") stands for "Black, indigenous, and people of color," and it is used as shorthand here to delineate the fact that this group is 100-percent non-white. As mentioned previously, we did not let the machine-learning algorithm see ethnicity or race at all for the purpose of creating the four dechurched evangelical profiles. Rather, that machine-learning algorithm only saw things like education, political and cultural preferences, doctrinal matters, and willingness to return to an evangelical church.[1] The fact that this completely non-white group emerged from the data clearly shows that racial/ethnic makeup has a profound correlation with attitudes, influences, beliefs, behaviors, and sense of belonging.

Jeremiah is written as a successful, middle-aged Black male to reflect the demographics of the group. These are highly educated, upwardly-mobile, affluent, non-white people who chose to regularly attend an evangelical church at some time in the past. The group itself is overwhelmingly male. The fact that they chose to worship in what was likely a white evangelical context introduces a lot of nuance into the story. Individuals in this group made their choices for a wide range of reasons. Certainly for some in this group, class appears to be a bigger cultural factor than race or ethnicity. For this reason,

---

1. The algorithm got to see twenty of the more than six hundred data points we have on each dechurched evangelical respondent.

we would urge caution in extrapolating this particular profile of the evangelically dechurched to encompass BIPOC in general.

The dechurched BIPOC group was the smallest subgroup by just a bit, representing 14 percent in our survey of those who have left evangelical churches. If that extrapolated to American adults, there could be 2 million people like Jeremiah. In our survey, they are 76 percent Black, 15 percent Hispanic, 5 percent Asian/Pacific Islander, and 4 percent other. They are 68 percent male and 32 percent female. Their average age at the time of this study was 52 years old (1971 birth year) and on average they dechurched twenty-five years ago (1998). They have by far the highest level of education of any of the five subgroups, and they are tied with the cultural Christians for highest income.

We were struck by how the group was overwhelmingly Black (76%) and male (68%). Over half of those surveyed in this group (52%) were Black men. Extrapolated there could be a million affluent and upwardly mobile Black men out there who, like Jeremiah, have left evangelical churches. These men are *by far* the most educated and affluent of any of the dechurched categories, not just among evangelicals, but of any religious tradition.

This group is disproportionately located in the Southeast in our survey with 38 percent living in that region. The concentrations of those in this group outside of the Southeast largely maps with the distribution patterns of the Great Migration of American descendants of slaves (ADOS) out of the South.

Regarding sexual orientation, in our survey, dechurched BIPOC are 96 percent heterosexual, 2 percent bisexual, and 1 percent homosexual, making them the second most heteronormative of the four evangelical clusters. The vast majority are also married (80%).

Jeremiah has been characterized with workaholic tendencies because no group works more than this one. An incredibly high 92 percent of dechurched BIPOC in our survey work full-time, with only an infinitesimal 1 percent being retired. This is noteworthy, given that their average age is 52 years old.

Somewhat counterintuitively, we discovered that this is also the most unrooted group, with a surprising 54 percent in our survey moved in the last year. They were the highest in every category of moving in the last year with 40 percent making an intracity move, 11 percent making an intrastate move, and 3 percent moving to another state.

Ideological Complexity and "Triple-Mindedness"

Jeremiah is all over the place politically, ideologically, and experientially. He occupies predominantly white cultural spaces due to his education, employment, and income. If you think about the weekly activities of the expensive private school, the elite neighborhood, and the workplace—all of them were overwhelmingly white cultural spaces. Further, he grew up with divergent parental influences regarding politics. There were significant differences between his mother's cultural norms as someone who is ADOS and his father's, which bore a certain type of Afro-Caribbean and Jamaican nuance. Jeremiah's backstory reveals what seminal African American scholar W. E. B. Du Bois called in 1903 "double consciousness":

> One ever feels his two-ness,—an American, a negro; two souls, two thoughts, two unreconciled strivings; two warring ideals in one dark body, whose dogged strength alone keeps it from being torn asunder.
>
> The history of the American Negro is the history of this strife,—this longing to attain self-conscious manhood, to merge his double self into a better and truer self. In this merging he wishes neither of the older selves to be lost.[2]

At a minimum, Jeremiah has to navigate the double consciousness, but perhaps for him there is actually a triple consciousness, since

2. W. E. B. Du Bois, *The Souls of Black Folk* (New York: Dover, 1994), 2.

he must navigate the ways the disparate influences of Mavis (ADOS), Glenroy (Afro-Caribbean), and white cultural spaces all intersect.

That triple consciousness reveals itself in many of the tensions and complexities in the attitudes of this particular group. What we see in the data is that dechurched BIPOC are center-left party-wise and policy-wise (abortion, COVID-19, foreign policy, gun control, global warming, same-sex marriage, and more). They had a low Christian nationalism score, but the majority (55%) also felt that "moving a conservative agenda was worth any price of supporting Trump." Surprisingly, 57 percent of this non-white group agreed that the January 6 riot at the US Capitol was "an effort by patriots to protect and restore our Christian nation." Furthermore, 52 percent agreed that "the US military should support Vladimir Putin and Russia in their special military operation in Ukraine."

Perhaps most surprising is the fact that half of the members of the dechurched BIPOC group feel that "racial problems in the US are rare, isolated situations." This unexpected consensus puts dechurched evangelical persons of color in second place out of the five groups in having a relatively positive view of racial tensions in our country. The only group with a more optimistic response to this particular question was the cultural Christians, with 54 percent in our survey expressing the belief that US racial conflicts are uncommon rather than widespread.

Jeremiah's triple-mindedness represents a confluence of these seemingly conflicted positions. He lives suspended between three worlds. He doesn't easily fit into boxes or labels due to the complexity of his interracial marriage, his many white-dominated cultural spaces, his father's military background, and the relative differences between Glenroy's and Mavis's backgrounds and perspectives. It is important that we not regard people monolithically, especially the dechurched BIPOC, when we seek to engage with them. If cultural differences are involved, a posture of listening and curiosity will serve you and them well.

Information Diet, Attitudes, and Relational Dynamics

Dechurched BIPOC are highly informed people. They read more books, have more wide-ranging news perspectives,[3] and spend more time on social media[4] than the other subgroups. When looking for advice, information, or a better perspective on some issue, dechurched BIPOC intentionally look to friends, parents, mentors, and books more than those in the other subgroups do.

Unfortunately, this group has had below-average experiences with US institutions across the board. While not totally despairing, their confidence scores were consistently low, with levels between 30 and 40 percent in all institutions, including the government, the economy, the police, and the education, judicial, and health care systems.

Mental health indicators are also low for dechurched persons of color. Tragically, they have the lowest scores of the five subgroups on their sense of identity, security, meaning, and purpose. Furthermore, their scores on anxiety, depression, and loneliness were also the worst by a small margin. However, they did fare a little better than others on suicidal thoughts, which may be related to the fact that they have the most close friendships[5] and the highest average number of people who truly know them.[6]

Doctrine, Beliefs, and Church Involvement

When it comes to primary doctrines of faith, dechurched BIPOC in our survey are relatively unorthodox. They scored the second lowest overall in their agreement with basic tenets of Christian theology, such as belief in the Trinity; the reliability of the Bible; the divinity/

---

3. CNN (27%), Fox News (27%), and MSNBC (14%).
4. Facebook (18 hours per week), YouTube (18 hours per week), Instagram (17 hours per week), and WhatsApp (18 hours per week).
5. On average 5.5 close friends.
6. On average 4.9 people who truly know them.

humanity of Jesus; Jesus' sinlessness, atonement, and resurrection; and his exclusivity as Savior. They scored slightly higher in our survey than cultural Christians on the belief that Jesus is the Son of God (13%) and in believing that the Bible is the literal word of God (29%). Only 52 percent of dechurched BIPOC believe in heaven, and 50 percent believe in hell. They have significant doubts about God's existence. They also don't exhibit a lot of religious behaviors, such as prayer, worship attendance, fasting, and devotional reading. Relative to the other groups, they had a lower rate of past involvement in church youth groups (20%) but higher involvement in church-based college ministry (25%) and campus ministry (18%).

The fact that Jeremiah showed some openness toward Catholicism during his time at Notre Dame helped to illustrate the fact that many dechurched BIPOC switched affiliations after dechurching. Catholicism is the most common landing spot for these formerly Protestant evangelicals (39%), with "other world religions" (14%), and "nothing in particular" (14%) being their next most likely destinations. Had our hypothetical character been Hispanic rather than Black, he would have been more likely to embrace Catholicism, with 15 percent of Latinos pivoting to the Catholic Church after leaving evangelical ones.

Sadly, those in the dechurched BIPOC group reported having cycled through far more congregations in their lifetime, at an average of 6.5 churches per person. That total is roughly double the averages of the other groups. While it is true that they move more frequently, they also seem to have felt less comfortable in evangelical churches. When we consider the big picture painted by all the other data on the dechurched BIPOC group, the tendency to church hop makes sense on many levels.

Why They Left

Like Jeremiah, the dechurched BIPOC group in our survey left church on average around the year 2000. They reported having a particularly difficult time staying in church during their transitions from high school age (13–17) to their postgraduation years (18–25) and also moving into the young professional years (26+).

When transitioning from their teens to their early twenties, the most difficult hurdles this group encountered about church were those detailed in figure 6.1.

Figure 6.1. Reasons for Leaving Church (18–25)

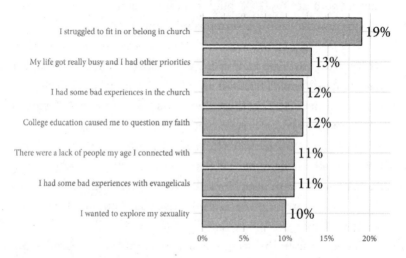

Clearly, dechurched BIPOC find it difficult to feel they still belong at church after high school. From their teens (13–17) to college age (18–25), we see a jump from 3 to 19 percent who reported struggling to fit in at their evangelical churches. This is the single largest jump of any factor of any group at any life transition. During the same time period, they also reported having had more negative experiences in the church (from 2% up to 11%) and having bad experiences with evangelicals (from 2% up to 12%).

In the transition from 18–25 to young professionals (26–39), their biggest challenges were those shown in figure 6.2.

Figure 6.2. Reasons for Leaving Church, Young Professionals (26–39)

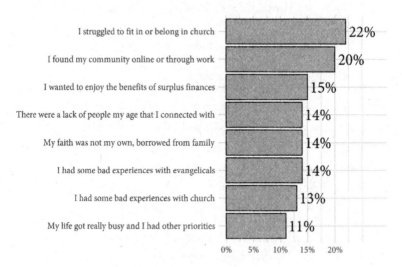

There was also a big relational shift for this group concerning where they find their core community. During the 18-to-25-year-old phase, only 8 percent say, "I found my community and relationships online or work," but this jumps to 20 percent during the young professional phase. In this new life station, it becomes much more likely that they would describe their faith as being borrowed from their family, from 6 to 14 percent.

In our survey, a number of things stood out as unique about the dechurched BIPOC subgroup. These five issues all made their top ten reasons for dechurching, while being absent or rarely on the other groups' top ten lists:

- Faith just wasn't working (19%).[7]
- I had other priorities for my time and money (18%).[8]

---

7. #6 for dechurched Catholics (11%).
8. #10 for cultural Christians (15%).

- Suffering changed my views of God and/or the congregation (18%).[9]
- I didn't see the congregation doing enough good in the community (16%).
- The messages were not relevant to my life (16%).

Another way this group stood out was in the influence their parents had on their church involvement. Unfortunately, parents play a more negative role in the dechurched BIPOC's decision to dechurch than for any other group. So what exactly is it that parents are doing to drive young adults of color away from church? Figure 6.3 lists what they claim are their biggest issues regarding their parents.

Figure 6.3. Parental Reasons for Leaving Church

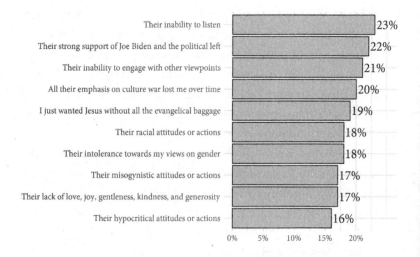

9. #4 for cultural Christians (17%).

The dechurched BIPOC group and the cultural Christians group experienced the most friction when it came to their parents and how that relationship impacted their decision to dechurch. When asked how parents could better engage with them in hopes of encouraging a return to church, respondents advised their parents to do these things:

- Try to listen better (37%).
- More consistently embody love, joy, gentleness, kindness, and generosity (36%).
- Change their views on gender (27%).
- Change their views on women in leadership (25%).
- Try to engage more charitably with other viewpoints (23%).
- Be less political (22%).

Many of these items are commonsense ways of exhibiting relational wisdom, but others are less intuitive. It is common sense that parents should be active listeners and seek the fruit of the Spirit. However, parents who are struggling with dechurched children (or grandchildren) should be more charitable and exercise more temperance when expressing potentially controversial viewpoints. Another way to think about this is leading with listening and curiosity. If you are strong and secure in your perspective, then alternative viewpoints should not cause you to be defensive or reactionary. A quiet, calm, and curious demeanor can be attractive and disarming. We will talk more about that in chapter 9, "Relational Wisdom."

Why They Would Be Willing to Return to an Evangelical Church

The good news is, 65 percent of BIPOC former evangelicals in our study are willing to return to an evangelical church, and only 5 percent of this group would *never* be willing to return. When asked why they might be persuaded to come back, their responses primarily center around social reasons and nostalgia.

The top reasons dechurched BIPOC in our survey say they would be willing to come back to church are provided in figure 6.4.

Figure 6.4. Reasons for Returning

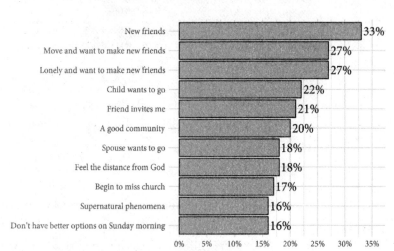

When we look at the reasons why dechurched BIPOC would be willing to return to church, the top seven reasons are all relational in some way. Whether those relational reasons surround making new friends, having loved ones who want to go, or needing a community of people, it is obvious that people similar to this profile are relationally hungry. You can also see in this group a residual spiritual sensitivity. Whether that involves feeling distant from God, missing church, or openness to the supernatural, spiritual interest still remains.

In many ways and like many of the other profiles, the reasons for being willing to return are just the photonegative of why the dechurched BIPOC left. Evangelicals both individually and institutionally failed this group of people, especially relationally, and even though well over two decades have passed, two-thirds are still willing to put that behind them and come back if we can relate in an understanding way.

What Can We Do?

Dechurched BIPOC as a group have many unique characteristics that extend far beyond race or ethnicity. Fortunately, these distinct qualities also produce a number of specific takeaways for those who want to better minister to this group.

Relational challenges have featured prominently in every group, but they are even more pronounced among the dechurched BIPOC. The need to have a sense of belonging and at least somewhat fit in has had a strong impact on their decisions about church and community. The negative encounters they've had with evangelicals and their churches were deal breakers for them, especially when they were eighteen to thirty years old.

Those churches who wish to earn back the trust of this group of estranged members must work to take responsibility for changing any hurtful attitudes and behaviors, such as putting political partisanship above relationship. We must improve our cultural and emotional intelligence and increase our understanding of and empathy for their specific experiences and needs.

As we saw in Jeremiah's story, many white evangelicals still lack a basic cultural competency. Our ignorance of the ways we alienate people of other races and ethnic backgrounds only exacerbates the already difficult underlying factors keeping them from our churches. This is especially true as differences in life station increase, such as being further separated by language, income, or even age. Not only the parents of this group, but any older Christians who want to serve a vital, healing role in the lives of younger, at-risk people of color must strive to be quick to listen, slow to speak, and embrace postures of curiosity and empathy toward different viewpoints.

This group needs people in their lives who will pursue deep friendship with them in spite of their frequent moves and long hours in high-powered and high-stress jobs. Traditional church programs are not enough. This might require thinking outside the traditional box and greater clarity on the changing needs and demographics. The goal is not merely to increase attendance or membership but to extend the love and gospel of Jesus Christ to those who make up a critical mission field right outside our doors. It may take extra effort to break through relationally, but as evangelists tasked with fulfilling the Great Commission, we must prioritize making those efforts. We must love our neighbors of all colors and backgrounds. If you are a member of the dominant culture, then this will require cultural humility on your part if you want to prioritize gospel mission above cultural preferences.

Don't forget that dechurched BIPOC are highly mobile, moving twice as often as other dechurched groups. Your church may have only a brief window of time to make a big impact on a person or household. One pastor we know in a highly mobile city often says his job feels like he is "hugging a parade as it is going by him." What if we all accepted the stewardship task of investing in people, knowing that we will give a lot of our heart to others whom we'll have to say a difficult goodbye to in the not-too-distant future? Many of us have benefited from people who have been loved well by other churches for brief periods of their life. If we all did this with a kingdom view in mind, God's kingdom would prolifically advance.

The value and priority of church membership already appears in decline among evangelicals. Often, following up with former members who have moved is barely on the radar. We'll talk more about this concept in chapter 8, "Reasons to Hope," but the low-hanging fruit here is simply to follow up when you hear that someone is moving or has moved. Call, check in, and ask if you can help them find a good local church in their new location. Given the amount of time this group spends online, social media and other digital strategies also provide an important opportunity for helping them stay within the care of a loving church family.

Finally, to better serve the dechurched BIPOC group, our evangelical churches need to have a greater focus on spiritual formation and doctrine. We have big opportunities for discipleship and catechesis. We need more churches that are confessional *and* missional. The dechurched BIPOC need people who care enough to listen to their questions and assuage those doubts that arose during their college years and early careers. They need to see firsthand the benefits of prayer and reading the Bible and to experience the joy of worshiping with people who love Christ and who love them.

Chapter 7

Dechurched Mainline Protestants and Catholics

CONOR IS A BLUE-COLLAR DIEHARD RED SOX FAN FROM THE GRITTY shores of South Boston, but now he lives in rural Tennessee.

He started going to Alcoholics Anonymous when his work buddy Sam invited him. Sam had just earned his ten-years-sober chip. That sounded like something Conor would like to have one day, so after his second meeting, Conor asked Sam to be his sponsor. Sam said he would be glad to sponsor him, and they made plans to meet for coffee later that week at the local diner.

At the diner, they made small talk for a few minutes, and then Sam asked, "I know you from work, obviously, but I don't know much personal stuff, like, do y'all have any kids?"

"Yeah, I got two kids, but they're both grown now, working and all."

"And your wife . . . Cynthia, right?"

"Good memory! Yeah, unfortunately, we just recently divorced. Well, it's actually been more like eighteen months now, so I guess not that recent."

Sam frowned, "Man, I didn't know. That is rough."

"I didn't mention it to anyone at work. I've been kinda checked out, I guess. Cynthia and I were married for twenty-seven years. Both grew up in Boston. We were high school sweethearts." It was obvious Conor was still feeling this loss deeply.

"So, did y'all meet at school? Church?" Sam asked.

"At school. I played varsity football, and she was a cheerleader. All-American fairytale, I guess," Conor's smile didn't quite reach his eyes. "We went to the same school but different churches."

"Oh, okay, I didn't know if you came from a church background or what," Sam admitted.

"Yeah, we did, and we still went, even after we were married. When the kids were little. Growing up, my family was Catholic. We went to mass every week. Cynthia was in the youth group over at the Episcopal church. Me, I was too focused on football and earning money working for my uncle to do youth group and all that."

Sam asked him, "How long have you worked in the nuclear power industry?"

"Well, see, Cynthia got pregnant right after I graduated, and as soon as we found out, we went and got married. Boston wasn't cheap, and it wasn't going to work out long term to live in my parents' basement with a new wife and baby. So my uncle . . . the one who I said I worked for in high school? He was in construction, and he helped build the nuclear power plant outside Boston back in the day. So he called up a buddy of his, and he got me down there."

"So they just hired you with no experience or anything?"

"You're probably a little too young to remember, but Chernobyl had just melted down around that time and Three Mile Island was still on everybody's mind, so I figure they were just glad to hire anybody who wasn't afraid they were gonna end up with radiation poisoning, the way the news was going on and on about the dangers and all."

"After y'all married, did you end up going to the Catholic church or the Episcopal church?" Sam asked.

"We did kind of a mishmash, I guess you would call it. We went to Holy Eucharist at the Episcopal church and then went over to Sunday evening mass at the Catholic church. That made both our families happy, and kept the peace in the marriage. For a while, anyway."

Sam nodded and filled his cup from the copper-colored carafe. "So how does a guy from the south side of Boston end up in backwoods Tennessee?" Sam asked.

"Well, even though the nuclear plant paid real good for a guy with a high school diploma, Boston was expensive and the neighborhood was rough. With two kids, me and Cynth knew we needed the money to go further than we could ever stretch it in the city."

"Did you know someone down here?"

"Yeah, I had a work buddy who had just transferred to the Watts Plant, and he was saying how much he liked Spring City, and the houses were a lot cheaper—at least back then they were in the '90s."

Sam smiled knowingly. "So how was that transition? Much of a culture shock for y'all? How long did it take for it to start to feel like home?"

"Honestly, I'm not sure it ever has completely felt like home. Here everyone is white, Protestant, Republicans. Some of 'em called us Yankees to our faces, and others just said it behind our backs. First time I heard that, I thought, *Whoa, I hate the Yankees as much as anybody.* I'm a hardcore Red Sox fan, you know? Then I figured out what they meant."

Conor's brow furrowed as he sorted through the memories. "I guess so? Maybe a slow, gradual thing? We were so focused on getting from one day to the next, you know, raising the kids, working. Things on the job were going well for me, but I felt the pressure of college looming in the near future, trying to save up for that. I took a lot of extra shifts, and I finally found some buddies at the pub to wind down with, and I started having a drink or two after work every night to take the edge off."

"Did Cynthia complain about your drinking or your long hours at work?"

"Nah, not really. She was all wrapped up in the kids and all their school stuff, sports stuff, and everything. It's not like my drinking increased that much right then. Like I said, it was just a slow drift going on during those years, with our marriage taking a back seat to the kids' needs and me burning the candle at both ends." Conor trailed off his story, and there was a lull in the conversation.

The waitress brought them some pie. Sam thanked her and slid a roll of silverware across the Formica tabletop to Conor.

"Why don't I tell you a little more about my own recovery, unless you're in a hurry to finish up and get home?" Sam offered.

Conor cut the tip off his slice of French silk. "I got nothing and nobody waiting for me at home, so you just have at it," Conor said, relieved to change the subject from him.

"As you know, I'm from here. Married a hometown girl and all. My life looked good from an outside view. But behind closed doors, I was numbing out with alcohol. My brothers and I had a difficult father. He was hard on our mom and on us, and I eventually had to deal with some of that leftover baggage working through the twelve steps."

"You never know what someone is dealing with privately," Conor nodded sympathetically.

"Exactly. Growing up, we went to church and looked like the perfect family, like you were talking about. My dad was even chairman of the deacons at the same Baptist church where my sponsor used to be a deacon. Small town life, right?" Sam laughed.

"Aw, man. So your pop, he was a real wolf in sheep's clothing, huh?" Conor said, scowling.

"It's easy to throw the baby out with the bathwater on this subject. When I got sober, I had to learn to tease apart the true faith of the Bible from any false practices or fake Christians I had encountered and hold on to the good stuff. For me, recovery and faith go hand-in-hand," he said. "That's why I asked you about church. Do you have one that can support you right now as you get sober?"

"Look, I'm gonna be real honest with you, kid." Conor rubbed his palms on his pants legs. "I don't know if I'll ever darken the doorstep of another church."

"Oh, okay. How come?"

"In early 2002, I got a phone call from my ma that just . . . let's just say it changed the rest of my life," he said. "She asked me if I had heard about the report in the *Globe* about the archdiocese. I said I hadn't. So Ma started talking about how she was worried because some of the stories coming out were really bad, and her and my dad even recognized the names of some of the priests who were involved. She went on and on, so by this time I had kind of tuned out what all she was saying. Then she finally blurted out, 'Jimmy, one of those priests touched Tommy.' That woke me up real quick."

Conor was looking down as he talked now, reliving the conversation in his mind. "So I asked her, 'What do you mean, Ma? What are you sayin' to me right now?'" He looked up at Sam, stricken. Through clenched teeth he said, "She told me our priest had sexually violated my brother."

"What? No. No. *No* . . ."

"Yeah. Turns out it was true. That monster *raped my kid brother.*"

Sam exhaled slowly, "I can't even imagine how hard that must have been for you to hear." They sat in silence for a long minute. Finally, Sam asked, "So . . . how did you guys deal with it, like, as a family?"

"I basically just shut down after Ma dropped that bomb that day. That was it for me; I was done with the Catholic Church forever. I didn't even want to go to the Episcopal church either. Just driving by the buildings made me feel sick in my gut."

"That makes sense," Sam said. "It's a normal reaction after something like that, to just shut down and try to avoid the painful stuff any way you can. We drink to just forget for a while."

"The thing is," Conor confessed in a quiet voice, "While I've been sitting here telling you all that, I've just now realized it was after I got the news about Tommy that my drinking got outta hand." His voice choked up. "I mean, I wanted to call Tommy, offer my support, I really did . . . " Conor swallowed hard, fighting back tears. He took a deep breath in through his nose. "I just couldn't make myself do it."

"I can see why you would be. That was beyond imagining. I am so sorry." Sam gave Conor a minute to breathe and calm down.

"So, after all that, you just shut down and didn't deal with any of it, not even with your brother?"

"It shames me to say it, but I never did. Not a word."

"Wow. So what happened then?"

"You know, the kids graduated and went off to college, and Cynthia and I got a divorce." He talked around a bite of pie. "It wasn't messy though. I think we would both say we still care very much for each other. We just can't live together."

"And you never went back to any kind of church, Catholic or otherwise?" Sam asked him.

"Cynthia, she kept going to the Episcopal church until after our youngest kid graduated. And, I mean, we both still believed in Jesus, God, and all of that. There were times when we would still pray, you know, separately. Not together. I mean, we both were still moral people. We think of ourselves as good people, you know? We still felt really strong against stuff like racism, lying, stealing, and so forth. But it was a private thing. We didn't need someone preaching at us every Sunday while the rest of the time they were off doing God knows what in private."

Sam nodded and took a deep breath. "Thanks for sharing all this with me, man. It makes sense. Lot of hurt there."

"Well, thanks, I guess," Conor said, shaking his head. "I never just up and told anybody all that before. Feels kinda good to get it all out."

Understanding the Dechurched
Mainline and Catholic

One of the more surprising results of our large quantitative study is how similar dechurched mainline Protestants[1] and Catholics are. The parallels are so remarkable that there is relatively little to distinguish between the two. Before we delve into the common elements of both groups, let's take a brief look at the handful of differences between the two groups.

Differences between Dechurched Mainliners and Catholics

The biggest difference in our survey between dechurched mainliners and Catholics was gender. While the Catholic group was only 48 percent female, the mainline dechurched group was 68 percent female.[2] That gender disparity was matched only by the 68 percent male demographic among the dechurched BIPOC evangelical group. Both of those figures should appear in flashing red lights, as they are significant outliers.

Our survey also revealed big differences according to region, with dechurched Catholics having the largest presence of any group in any tradition in the Northeast. A significant 29 percent of dechurched Catholics were in the Northeast, with mainliners being the next highest in that region at 17 percent and no evangelical subgroup exceeding 13 percent.

Dechurched Catholics in our survey had a slightly higher marriage rate (55%) than their mainline counterparts (47%). Both groups included a significant population of retirees, but mainliners had a

---

1. Note that "mainline" is short for "mainline Protestants," which is comprised primarily by the following seven denominations: American Baptist Churches, Christian Church (Disciples of Christ), the Episcopal Church, the Evangelical Lutheran Church in America, the Presbyterian Church (USA), the United Church of Christ, and the United Methodist Church.

2. It is unclear to us as to why, and this warrants further research.

higher percentage (41%) than Catholics did (31%). Both groups had a dearth of full-time workers, but mainliners had the lowest number (25%), whereas Catholics had a bit more (36%).

Like Cynthia, mainliners had a high rate of youth group involvement (36%) compared to Catholics (17%). Dechurched Catholics' clergy, congregation, friends, community, and state were unilaterally less supportive of Donald Trump than the mainline dechurched by an average of 8 percent and were lower than all evangelical subgroups. Dechurched Catholics were more likely to cite political friction, misogyny, and desiring more sexual freedom as reasons why they dechurched than the dechurched mainline group. Compared to Catholic respondents, the mainline dechurched folks were more likely to cite personal suffering and the church not doing enough good in the community as reasons for leaving.

Now that we've covered the handful of differences between dechurched mainliners and dechurched Catholics, the rest of the data shows only minimal differences between the two groups. For this reason, we will look at the remaining factors together.

Doctrine, Beliefs, and Church Involvement

We would have expected greater doctrinal disagreements between dechurched mainliners and dechurched Catholics, but we didn't see much difference on several key doctrines.

These figures were similar to dechurched cultural Christians and dechurched BIPOC evangelical groups but were significantly lower than mainstream evangelical and exvangelical respondents. Catholics and mainliners looked similar to each other and to the cultural Christians and dechurched BIPOC groups with the exception of the exclusivity of Jesus among dechurched Catholics. Both mainline and Catholic groups had a lower view of the Bible than any other group.

Overall there does seem to be a high correlation between one's view of the Bible and the other doctrinal questions. Those who had a high view of the Bible scored highly on other central doctrines. A lower view of the Bible seems to have eroded belief in many of the other theological positions. There does seem to be a lot of opportunity in mainline and Catholic contexts to use the historic creeds and confessions here and to try and instill a greater confidence in the Bible.

Figure 7.1. Theological Positions of Dechurched Mainline/Catholic

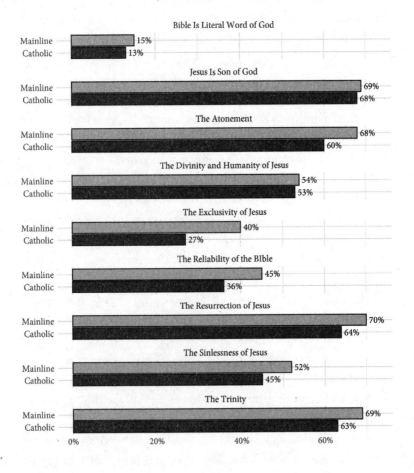

Dechurched mainline and Catholic groups in our survey both lean center-left to left with respect to political affiliation and policy. Both groups are deeply allergic to Christian nationalism, Donald Trump, the Capitol riots of January 6, 2021, racism, and misogyny. The groups had virtually identical media diets of 29 percent broadcast news, 21 percent Fox News, and 13 percent CNN.

Why Did They Leave?

The biggest reasons why mainliners and Catholics dechurched are cited in figures 7.2 and 7.3.

Moving had a greater impact on dechurching for mainliners than it did for Catholics. This is somewhat unexpected because neither group moves much, with 87 percent of dechurched mainliners and 85 percent of dechurched Catholics not moving in the last year. Apart from this outlier, most of the top eight reasons for dechurching are held in common between both groups and at similar levels.

Figure 7.2. Reasons for Leaving Church (Mainline)

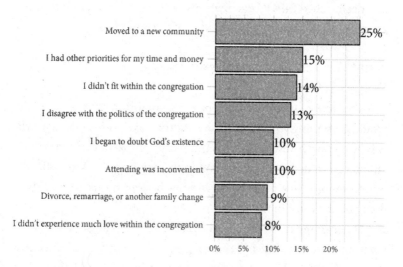

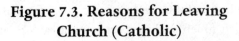

Figure 7.3. Reasons for Leaving Church (Catholic)

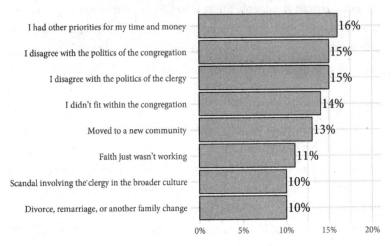

The greatest points of friction for dechurched mainline and Catholic groups surround politics, belief, use of time, and life change. Given the low orthodoxy score—similar to the cultural Christians and dechurched BIPOC evangelicals—we question what percentage actually possess a saving knowledge of the gospel.

What Kind of Church Would They Be Willing to Return To?

The top reasons why dechurched mainliners and Catholics would be willing to return to the church have a lot to do with the way the church interacts with the world. In particular, they have an interest in doing tangible good in the community. After all, why would you go back to a church if other organizations are out there doing better work in the community?

One can see from figure 7.4 that the very top priority that both traditions are looking for is strong social programs, followed by strong educational programs and activities focused on dialogue. By contrast lower values are associated with outreach, spiritual practices, and salvation.

Figure 7.4. Prioritize What a Congregation Should Do

1 = Most Important; 7 = Least Important

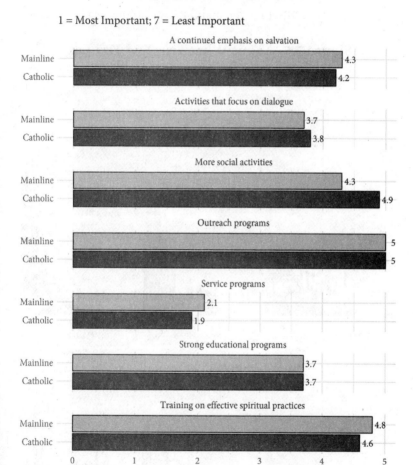

Comparing Dechurched Mainliners, Catholics, and Evangelicals

Our study showed there are large differences in age as well as when mainliners, Catholics, and evangelicals dechurched. Catholics dechurched on average at age 31, whereas mainliners averaged age 32. However, mainliners are the oldest of the groups, at an average age of 58. Catholics had an average age of 53, and evangelicals had an average age of 44.

Mainliners were the first group to dechurch more rapidly, starting in the early 1970s. Like the mainliners, Catholics had a flattened

Figure 7.5. About What Year Did You Last Attend a Congregation a Few Times?

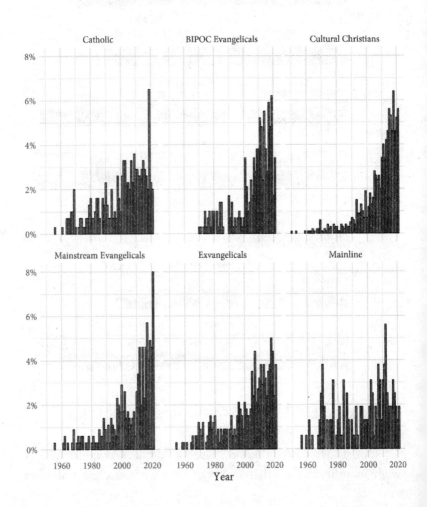

and linear rate of dechurching. Every dechurched evangelical sub-group, however, had a much more rapid rise, looking more like a spike than a consistent straight-line increase. There are notable spikes surrounding COVID-19 for Catholics and mainstream evangelicals in particular. To a lesser extent but still noteworthy, there seem to be some spikes on either side of the 2016 election cycle as well. So dechurching was first a mainline phenomenon, then a Catholic one, and now an evangelical one. It is difficult to say if we have reached peak dechurching yet. Eventually, in a manner not dissimilar from a pandemic spike, dechurching will have to slow down because there won't be enough people who are still churched to maintain the spike.

It is noteworthy that both the dechurched mainline and Catholic groups in our survey were far less prone to prosperity gospel (31% prosperity average score versus 58% for evangelicals). Further, both mainline and Catholic groups were less prone to Christian nationalism (20% Christian nationalism average score versus 29% for evangelicals). This is important when it comes to ministering more effectively to these groups and should serve as a critique of evangelicalism.

Dechurched evangelicals have overrepresentation in the Southeast, and mainline and Catholics are overrepresented in the Northeast. Dechurched evangelicals have significantly higher incomes than their mainline and Catholic counterparts. Age, gender, working full-time percentage, and education all play a significant role in that gap.

One counterintuitive and fascinating insight is that regardless of tradition, increased education *decreases* the likelihood of dechurching. You have likely heard the critique that universities are destroying people's faith and replacing it with secularism, but that isn't borne out by the data at all (see fig. 7.6).

According to our study, the more education a person has, the less likely that person is to dechurch. It is particularly noteworthy that only 11 percent of evangelicals in our study who went to graduate school have dechurched. Conversely, this means that those with less education are at greater risk of dechurching. We ought to be mindful and increasingly inclusive of those with less education, realizing there might be greater cultural distance due to differences in education, class, or perspective.

Figure 7.6. Percent Dechurched by Education and Tradition

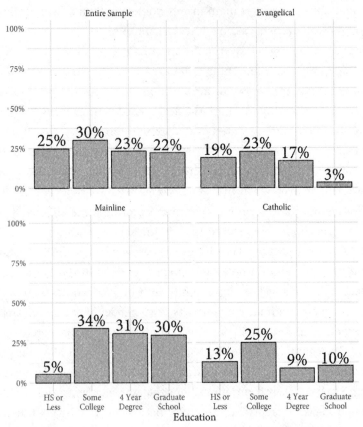

Politically, dechurched evangelicals lean center-right, whereas mainline and Catholic counterparts lean center-left. These dynamics also bear themselves out in policy preferences on things like abortion, COVID-19, foreign policy, gun control, global warming, same-sex marriage, and more.

Big differences exist in ethical priorities between still-churched evangelicals, dechurched evangelicals, and their mainline and Catholic counterparts (see fig. 7.7).

Figure 7.7. Which of the Following Standards and Practices Do You Seek to Follow in Good Faith?

Reasons Given	Overall Evangelical Dechurched	Dechurched Mainline	Dechurched Catholic	Still Churched Evangelicals ONLY
Avoid discrimination based on race	74%	96%	93%	93%
Avoid discrimination based on religion	75%	95%	90%	92%
Providing financially and/or practically for the poor and oppressed	71%	69%	69%	86%
Caring practically for immigrants, refugees, or otherwise displaced persons	66%	62%	65%	75%
Don't have an abortion	59%	48%	43%	77%
Avoid pornography	65%	68%	54%	84%
Avoid abuse of drugs and alcohol	69%	82%	79%	89%
Attend worship services	51%	23%	33%	88%
Pray regularly	64%	70%	64%	92%
Donate to house of worship	53%	31%	35%	85%
Don't lie	71%	93%	85%	91%
Don't steal	73%	97%	93%	96%
Don't be greedy	71%	91%	91%	94%
Read a holy book (e.g., the Bible) regularly	55%	35%	32%	82%

The differences in figure 7.7 are rather stark in the categories of "Avoid discrimination based on race," "Avoid discrimination based on religion," "Don't lie," "Don't steal," and "Don't be greedy." It is interesting to note that still-churched evangelicals fared better than one might expect, given much of the negative press in more recent years. That doesn't mean there isn't work to do to invalidate some of those critiques, but it does appear worth pointing out.

How to Minister to These Groups

Both dechurched mainliners and dechurched Catholics will be difficult to minister to and may require years of consistent and patient relationship. Both need to see a gospel that isn't just true but is also good and beautiful. They will likely need to see the gospel tangibly demonstrated before they have much interest in it being proclaimed. In our story, Sam is an excellent example of what this looks like. Sam hit rock bottom and has been profoundly changed by Jesus in his effort to find lasting sobriety. Conor desperately needs Sam in his life on multiple fronts, and Sam needs to patiently walk with him through addiction, grief, and loss from the divorce.

Doctrinally speaking, the core tenets of the faith and/or the gospel itself seem relatively unclear to most of the dechurched groups except the DMEs and the exvangelicals. It is possible that many lack a saving faith. We need to be showing them a gospel that is good, true, and beautiful because what some have seen called "gospel" in their former churches may not be real.

Most of these groups will tune out those who have difficulty separating their faith and politics, especially in the vein of Christian nationalism, Trumpian sentiments, xenophobia, misogyny, culture warring, and the prosperity gospel. Both groups may see these things as being out of step with the Sermon on the Mount. We will not be effective in ministering to either of these groups without both the gospel *and* the ethics of the kingdom. We need to be confessional and missional at the same time. Thus, we will spend an entire chapter (chapter 13) exploring what that looks like.

This is the final vignette that emerged from the data about profiles of the dechurched. But our work is far from over. Now that we've heard from the dechurched about who they are and why they left, we have a lot of work ahead of us answering the question "Now what?" We will spend the rest of the book examining the best things we can do to learn, grow, strengthen our own faith, be healthier, be more effective, mitigate future loss, and perhaps see a number of people return from any of these profiles or backgrounds.

Part 3

Engaging the Dechurched

Chapter 8

Reasons to Hope

ON MAY 10, 1940, THE GERMANS LAUNCHED A BLITZKRIEG ATTACK ON the Netherlands and Belgium, and in just five days they broke through the French defenses on their way to the English Channel, surrounding four hundred thousand Allied soldiers and the bulk of the British forces. Many historians agree that this could well have meant victory for Germany if they had captured or killed these soldiers who were no more than sitting ducks on the shore of Dunkirk, France.

But what looked like total defeat turned into victory for the Allied forces as, for the next eight days, naval and civilian boats made the sixty-mile voyage across the English Channel to retrieve the lion's share of these troops. Even though the battle was lost, the successful rescue of these troops allowed them to reassess and reorganize, and morale in England soared after Churchill's famous speech to the House of Commons: "We shall go on to the end . . . we shall fight on the seas and oceans, we shall fight with growing confidence and growing strength in the air, we shall defend our Island, whatever the cost may be, we shall fight on the beaches . . . we shall fight in the hills; we shall never surrender."[1] What at first

---

1. Winston Churchill, "Speech on the Evacuation at Dunkirk," Encyclopedia.com, https://www.encyclopedia.com/arts/encyclopedias-almanacs-transcripts-and-maps/speech-evacuation-dunkirk.

looked like a total loss renewed and reinvigorated the Allied forces to win the war.

As our data poured in on the Great Dechurching, one truth became increasingly clear: what looks like defeat to many could really be the beginning of something special. Tens of millions of people may be leaving the church, and more than eighty-six churches may be closing every week, but if we have eyes to see it, there is actually much reason to hope. We need to come to grips with some hard realities inside the church, but there are ways to win many of these people back. Some things are outside of our control, but others aren't. Success will require fruitful engagement with the things within our control without compromising the doctrines we hold most important. To put an even finer point on it, it is in the appropriate application of our doctrines where the lowest hanging fruit lies.

As we pointed out in chapter 2, 51 percent of the dechurched evangelicals we surveyed said they think they *will* one day return to church. Eighteen percent are "very willing," and 33 percent are "somewhat willing." This could be the single most unexpected and hopeful piece of data we found in our entire study. The opportunity before the church cannot be overstated. The question is, will we embrace it?

In this chapter, we will highlight the hopeful findings from our research for local churches and ministries to process in their local contexts. We have divided these observations into the sociological categories of belief, belonging, and behavior.

RYAN BURGE: When social scientists think about religion, they typically categorize religiosity in three ways: behavior, belief, and belonging. Behavior is measured through things like church attendance or amount of offering donated to a religious organization. Belief is assessed through asking questions about what a respondent believes about the existence of God, heaven, or hell. Belonging is more about social affiliations; a survey asks about a person's current religion, if any. The person taking the survey can say they are Protestant, Jewish, atheist, or some other choice from a menu of about a dozen options.

What is often overlooked is that when people say they no longer go to church or affiliate with a religious institution, that doesn't mean they leave all vestiges of religion behind. For instance, among those who say they are "nothing in particular" when it comes to their religious belonging, a third still say religion is "somewhat" or "very important" to them. They left the religious label behind but not their belief.

In the same way, a lack of church attendance doesn't necessarily mean someone has given up on the idea of God. Among those who report never attending church in the General Social Survey, the share who don't believe in God is about 20 percent. But the share of these never attenders who say they believe in God without any doubts is also about 20 percent.

Despite the fact that about 40 percent of Americans never attend church and 30 percent say they have no religious affiliation, just one in ten Americans says God does not exist or that we have no way to know if God exists. Religious belief is stubborn in the United States, and while someone may not act on that belief by going to a house of worship on Sunday morning, that doesn't mean they think their spiritual life is unimportant.

Belief

Early in our research, it was disorienting to realize how orthodox the dechurched still are in their beliefs. This brought equal parts hope and confusion. Sixty-eight percent of dechurched evangelicals

(DE), 69 percent of dechurched mainliners (DM), and 63 percent of dechurched Roman Catholics (DRC) all still believe in the Trinity. The divinity of Jesus (64% DE, 54% DM, 53% DRC) is still a strongly held view, as well as his sinlessness (61% DE, 52% DM, 45% DRC). Dechurched evangelicals still hold to primary doctrines like the atonement (65%), the resurrection (67%), the exclusivity of Jesus (62%), and the reliability of the Bible (61%). Dechurched mainline Christians hold similar numbers, as do dechurched Roman Catholics, except on the exclusivity of Jesus (40% DM, 27% DRC) and the reliability of the Bible (45% DM, 36% DRC).

Around two-thirds of the dechurched Christians we surveyed across tradition still believe evil forces are working in this world, including a literal devil. Fewer than 10 percent of the dechurched evangelicals we studied believe Jesus is a fictional character, while just a slightly higher percentage (20% DE, 5% DM, 4% DRC) believe Jesus was real but not special in any supernatural way. More than half of the dechurched we studied believe the Bible is a God-inspired book they can trust and believe in a literal heaven and hell. An astonishing 85 percent of dechurched evangelicals still pray to the God of the Bible.

We would be wise not to interact with the dechurched as we might with our unchurched friends, assuming they have no faith. Likely, their primary doctrinal convictions may well align with ours. Rather, we need to show them how the convictions they already hold apply to and should affect their lives. So what does this look like?

In our city, we have been encouraged by conversations surrounding belief with the dechurched. Not only is there a familiarity with our core doctrines but a general embracing of them as well. These conversations happen naturally over the dinner table or even at the gym in the context of relationships and trust. In almost every conversation we can think of with a dechurched person who is still largely orthodox (unless church trauma is involved), the person has expressed not only a knowledge that they should return to church but also a willingness to do so.

In 2020 my (Jim's) rhythms were upended, and exercising (something I have been fairly consistent at over the years) became nonexistent. I knew I should get back to the gym. I missed the relationships I had there. I missed being physically and emotionally healthy. I could see my anxiety levels rising and feel my body deteriorate. But I didn't go back. The problem wasn't in my beliefs. The problem was in my motivation and the knowledge of how my entire lifestyle would have to be altered. My bedtime would have to change, my alarm clock would have to change, and my eating would have to change. I knew I would go back, but each week I put it off one more week. I didn't need someone to tell me to go back to the gym; I needed someone to nudge me—to invite me back with them. And that is exactly what happened.

We believe a similar thing is needed with dechurched people who have maintained orthodox beliefs. Going back to church will upend their new Sunday morning rhythms. It will affect Saturday nights. It will mean prioritizing new relationships. But many dechurched individuals already think they will do it again one day. That day will perpetually remain tomorrow until someone invites them back to the community of God's people. If there is one single application from our research that you walk away with, please let it be this: invite your dechurched friends back to a healthy church with you. But unlike a simple nudge to go back to the gym, we would do well to open the doors our homes and chairs at our table. We aren't just telling them they should go back to church; we are inviting them into our lives, which includes church.

Belonging

Belonging (or lack thereof) is the primary pain point many dechurched feel. Of all the things people said would make them likely to return, this is the greatest felt need. We asked two vital questions to understand the animating concerns of the dechurched: What made you leave? And what would entice you to come back? The answers to these questions show us opportunities in front of us in this area of belonging.

Why did the dechurched leave? Some in our study left simply because they moved (19% DE, 25% DM, 13% DRC). They moved to a new city, hit the ground running, and developed new rhythms and friendships that changed their Sunday-morning patterns. This is also true for those who stopped going to church during the pandemic and never came back (13% DE, 7% DM, 8% DRC). Most dechurched evangelicals still worship online (which is more common among evangelicals anyway), but they do so at their convenience. Many evangelical churches now call their online worship services "on demand," and that is exactly what people are choosing to do. What is intended as a new front door is often having the opposite effect by helping the dechurched leave through the back door. Our research showed that physically going to a church in our consumerist digital age has become inconvenient, and many people have concluded that they have other priorities for their time and money.

As we said in chapter 2, these are the casually dechurched. No abuse or scandal sent them packing—no overarching, animating concern. They just stopped going to church and realized they prefer their new Sunday morning activities. They found another place to go, but in many cases, they did not find the sense of belonging they left behind.

The dechurched casualties left more intentionally. Some left because they didn't feel like they fit in (14% DE, 14% DM, 14% DRC) or because their friends didn't go with them (12% DE, 4% DM, 4% DRC). Others left because they didn't feel loved by their congregation (14% DE, 8% DM, 9% DRC) or because of a family change like divorce or remarriage (12% DE, 9% DM, 10% DRC), and they did not have the community in their church to overcome the difficulties of that change. Millions of people have left church simply because they desired to worship with people they knew and felt loved by but didn't experience that in their context. They desire to worship in a community where they feel like they belong.

What would it take to entice these people back? They told us. The desire to make new friends in general (28%) would be enough for some, but others would only desire those new friends after a move (18%) or if they became lonely (20%). For others, all it would take is a friend inviting them (17%) or finding a good community (17%). Some would go back if their child (16%) or spouse (18%) invited them. Finding a good pastor (18%) or a church they like (14%) would be enough for many. These are not high or unreasonable bars for a Christian community.

As church leaders, it's tempting to point the finger at the dechurched and their lack of commitment or discipline (which may in fact be an issue). But what if we instead held a mirror up to ourselves and asked what the Bible says about belonging in a Christian community? What are we doing to foster it in our churches? It's a sad indictment on the church that so many people find a more compelling and rich community around their children's sports teams, paddle boarding clubs, and the gym than in church.

Church is not an event; it is a family. It's not a perfect family, but it is a real spiritual family. We are, in some mysterious way, all grafted together into Jesus' body. This is a doctrine called *Christus totus*, the whole Christ. Christ is composed of both the person of Jesus and the church, which is the very body of Jesus. We are a part of who Jesus is, which makes genuine Christian belonging something we cannot find outside of the church.

We can find great community in our golf groups, social clubs, or children's schools, but that community is different from the belonging we find in a healthy church. It is not surprising that the dechurched indicate higher levels of anxiety, depression, and loneliness than those who immerse themselves in their faith community. One of Jesus' main aims for Christians is that we would increasingly be conformed into his image in the process of sanctification. While good friends, prayer groups, and even Bible studies help this process, if these events are detached from the local church, they just won't provide all the resources Jesus intends for us to have. In the local church we are given worship in song and teaching, corporate prayer, care and oversight, opportunities to serve, and the sacraments (or ordinances) of Communion and baptism. We are blessed by having to know and love people who are not like us—people who, outside the church, would not be in our lives.

So, the challenge is first to ask ourselves if our church operates more like an event or a family. Are we offering believers the full breadth of Christian belonging, or are we lowering the spiritual bar to accommodate the isolated and separated culture we live in? The widespread commodification of church as a spiritual good and service has led millions to ask what they can get from a church instead of what they can provide when, counterintuitively, it is in our provision for the church that we actually receive so many blessings. If church leaders are simply working to give attenders the best experience with the least amount of sacrifice, then why would they do anything more than drop in virtually when they have time? We must ask more of them. What we call them with is what we call them to.

But we can fall off the other side of this horse as well. We can work hard to provide an environment of community without the core Christian doctrines that make us Christian as these doctrines could create division in that community. We believe this is behind many who have dechurched because "the church had no real answers to their questions." When it becomes hard to distinguish a church family from other community-based groups, we lose the substantive relational depth God intends for his people. If all a church is good for is drawing people together as a community, why not do that with something more fun, like playing on a team or getting together with friends at a bar? If people can experience essentially the same feeling of community in these other places, why would we be surprised when people leave the church for those other groups?

Second, if we are experiencing the belonging Jesus intends for his people, are we calling our friends into it as well? Are you seeing a repeated pattern here? We hope so. As a church, we have what people desire, and our study shows they do see their desire for it.

Behavior

It's one thing to believe something; it's another to do it. Millions of Americans believe smoking is bad for their health but don't quit. Millions believe they should eat healthier but don't. One of the first things we noticed from our data was a similar inconsistency between what people believe and what they do. Fifty-one percent of dechurched evangelicals believe it is important to attend religious services but don't do it. That number is smaller but still significant among the dechurched mainline (23%) and dechurched Roman Catholics (33%). As we have mentioned, it is good news that many of the dechurched we interact with already believe they should be in church. The challenge for us is to listen and understand where the disconnect is between what they believe and what they practice. In chapter 12, "Spiritual Formation and the Dechurched," we will flesh out how to address some of the common reasons people choose not to go to church, but for now, we want to highlight the fact that many of the dechurched people in our lives don't need to be convinced that regular church attendance has value; they need to be encouraged to do what they already know they should.

The more complex behavioral issue is that of sexual ethic. Eleven percent of the dechurched evangelicals in our study indicated that the church was too restrictive of their sexual freedom. More than one in ten dechurched evangelicals choose not to attend a church that disagrees with their sexual behavior. While a deep dive into how to engage sexual ethics is beyond the scope of this book, we do want to point out that many of the people who dechurched over this issue are simply products of the church's inability to engage this issue well. Many churches are guilty of oversimplifying and even shaming people who don't understand the why behind the what in regard to sexual ethics. We've failed to engage their behavior via their hearts by speaking more than we listen, being harsh and insensitive, or on the opposite end of the spectrum, failing to address the issue at all because we are too concerned about pushing people away.

The issue of behavior goes both ways, though. We not only have the challenge of addressing behaviors outside the church; we also have to address them inside the church. Many of the dechurched we studied cited hypocrisy in the church as one of the reasons they dechurched. They indicated that they would be more than happy to return to a church that is flourishing by living out a consistent biblical ethic. Many of these people hold to the same doctrines but have become disappointed with the church's application of that ethic by not advocating passionately for biblical equality or against injustice. They desire the church to be the first to voice a biblical ethic to this fallen world, and that would be a compelling reason to return.

We also learned from our study that parents matter. In 2016 about 39 percent of Generation Z were nones (those with no religious affiliation in particular). Today that is up to 44.4 percent. We will cover this in more detail in chapter 10, "The Missed Generational Handoff," but for the purposes of addressing behavior, we asked the dechurched what advice they would have given their parent(s) that might have encouraged their faith and church attendance. We learned that simply listening better and more consistently embodying the fruit of the Spirit in interactions with children can change everything.

Belief, Belonging, and Behavior Are Connected

The Christian life is holistic. Our beliefs create belonging and dictate behavior. To prioritize one or two of these elements over the others is to fundamentally miss some part of the Christian faith. In fact, it is impossible to hold any two at the exclusion of the third. If we claim to believe and belong but our behavior is lacking, our faith is dead according to James 2. Our behavior shows a shortcoming in our belief. The apostle Paul, in his letter to the church in Corinth, addressed the issue of a man who claimed to be a believer and belonged to the church but was sleeping with his stepmother. Paul made it clear that this behavior should not be tolerated. He went so far as to tell the church that this man needed to be cast out in order to feel the conviction of his sin and repent.

If we claim to believe and behave but do not belong, we become a lone ranger Christian. While we have a category for shut-ins and other challenging circumstances, the Bible seems fairly clear that we are a people who gather together physically. Our lack of belonging is in itself a behavioral issue. The author of Hebrews tells us not to neglect meeting together. In every city where the gospel was preached in Acts, the new believers were connected to a local church. We are given dozens of "one anothers" in Scripture that can only be carried out as we belong to a local church. When we neglect the Bible's exhortations to belong, we can become stagnant and dull in our faith.

If we claim to belong and behave but do not hold to the fundamental beliefs of our faith, we don't belong to the faith. That may be fine for the Elks Lodge, but Paul, writing to the church in Corinth, said, "For I delivered to you as of first importance what I also received: that Christ died for our sins in accordance with the Scriptures, that he was buried, that he was raised on the third day in accordance with the Scriptures, and that he appeared to Cephas, then to the twelve. Then he appeared to more than five hundred brothers at one time, most of whom are still alive, though some have fallen asleep. Then he appeared to James, then to all the apostles. Last of all, as to one untimely born, he appeared also to me" (1 Cor. 15:3–8). The very thing that creates Christian belonging is our belief.

Our task in reaching out to the dechurched is about more than displaying the inconsistencies in our friends' lives. Our task is to display the richness of what Jesus offers his people in believing a gospel that creates a sense of belonging we can experience nowhere but in the church and a behavior that will allow us to live in line with and more fully experience the God who created us.

A Hopeful Future Can Require Hard Decisions

A hard reality we'll need to face is that some churches can pivot and reorganize to embody belief, belonging, and behavior as we were designed to, but others cannot. But that doesn't mean there is no hope. There are many ways churches can bless the kingdom in unexpected ways. For every three churches that closed in 2019, a new one started.[2] That may seem like losing math to many, but new churches have new life. Church plants are often much more effective at reaching the lost than older churches. In a Lifeway study making this claim, Ed Stetzer, who was at that time executive director of Lifeway Research, said, "In winning new converts to Christ, church plants are light-years ahead of the average church because of their focus on

---

2. "Protestant Church Closures Outpace Openings in U.S.," Lifeway Research, May 25, 2021, https://research.lifeway.com/2021/05/25/protestant-church-closures-outpace-openings-in-u-s/.

reaching the unchurched."[3] New believers are often the only way a new church can survive.

If your church is a stable, older church, are you engaged in planting new churches in your area? Are you not only willing but also planning to give money and people to that end? If your church seems unable to make this pivot, might it be better to bless a young church plant by bringing them into your established facility to worship when your church is not meeting? Or would you consider even giving them your building and joining them?

Let me contrast two dying churches in our area that represent many other churches I (Jim) know personally. Church A had its heyday just twenty-five years ago as it ran five worship services on the weekend and welcomed more than two thousand people each week. Now, as deficiencies have grown in the areas of belief, belonging, and behavior, the church has dwindled to about one hundred on Sunday. Church B was never as large as church A, but it has also taken a downward turn for the past twenty years. Church B has deficiencies in what they believe, but their belonging (even if they are small) seems to be quite strong. The leadership of church A seems to have its head in the sand as people continue to leave. They own their building outright and have endowments to pay a basic staff, but the church's future is clear. The congregation will continue to leave and die, commercial developers will come, and the church that used to be a light in the city will fade out completely.

Church B on the other hand, who also owns a great facility, has acknowledged that it cannot make the shifts necessary to continue, and they have invited a young, thriving church plant to use and eventually take over their facilities. The dying church, in its last breath, is giving this new church what it needs to live a long life. All may seem lost if our vision is dominated by our own small kingdom, but so

3. Lisa Green, "New Churches Draw Those Who Previously Didn't Attend," Lifeway Research, December 8, 2015, https://research.lifeway.com/2015/12/08/new-churches-draw -those-who-previously-didnt-attend/.

much is gained when we see our local church in view of God's large kingdom. Churches can win even in death.

Over two thousand years ago, as Jesus died on the cross, all seemed lost to his disciples. They felt like they had wasted three years. They went back to the lives they knew before Jesus. It would be hard to imagine the loss, defeat, and confusion they felt. But what looked like the ultimate defeat was all a part of Jesus' plan for victory. Three days later, they would see that. The same Jesus who resurrected from the dead and promised to be with us always now resides in us in the form of his Holy Spirit. Jesus declared that the gates of hell will not prevail against the church. As hopeful as this data is, our hope is in Jesus, in his power, and in his glory. Jesus has brought us into his mission for the redemption of his people and each of us individually as local churches play a divinely vital role. There is hope. It comes through both individual and corporate introspection. It requires coming alongside the dechurched as friends, not projects. It requires an examination of the belief, belonging, and behavior in our churches. It requires a kingdom perspective. But we believe deeply that if we do these things, there is much to hope for, and this season of loss could contribute to some of the greatest fruit in the American church to date.

Chapter 9

Relational Wisdom

WHEN WE ZOOM ALL THE WAY OUT AMONG ALL 40 MILLION PEOPLE
who have dechurched, one problem that becomes clear from our
survey data is relational incompetence in the ways both churched
individuals and churches themselves relate to persons at risk of
dechurching.

When we consider all the profiles in part 2 of this book, one
thing that sticks out is that many of the reasons why people left had
strong relational components. Whether they experienced a lack of
love, trouble fitting in, political disagreements, or other relational
factors, they often faced substantive relational challenges. The good
news about relational challenges being a significant factor is that we
can always grow in maturity and wisdom in terms of how we relate
to others. That is, the ways in which people experience us are within
our control, and we can purposefully develop ourselves.

Our cultural moment is evolving rapidly. The tectonic plates
of power are shifting historic alliances and allegiances, and these
macro-cultural and macro-sociological trends are changing the
ways people relate on the interpersonal level. These dynamics are
in play both inside and outside the church. As a result, the way we

should interact with those who have dechurched in the twenty-first century is also evolving rapidly. We have a gospel that is true, good, and beautiful, but the gospel emphasis in the twentieth century was largely on the gospel being true. This made sense as the Western world responded to the questions of modernity. Over the last fifty years, it appears fewer people are asking, "Is Jesus true?" and more are asking, "Is Jesus good?" and "Is Jesus beautiful?" People are asking more pragmatic, existential, and aesthetic questions as post-modernity, secularism, and other complex sociological, economic, political, psychological, and technological forces have them increasingly fractured culturally, relationally, and individually. People are longing for a better self, city, country, and world, and nobody seems to have the answers.

This shift in questions has been felt more acutely over the last several years, and we would be wise to navigate it deftly by growing in some critical competencies. Possessing these competencies will be increasingly important for having influence, leading effectively, and pastoring. To grow in relational wisdom and relational maturity, we must possess at least six key awarenesses—of God, of self, of others, of our emotions, of how others perceive us, and of culture.[1]

God-Awareness

The opening paragraph of John Calvin's *Institutes of the Christian Religion* begins with this profound insight: "Nearly all the wisdom

---

1. This entire chapter came out of hours of conversations with Jonathan Prudhomme. I (Mike) wrote the outline of this chapter, we (Mike and Jonathan) ideated this chapter originally to be published as an article, and Jonathan wrote most of the article. After writing it we both felt it actually made more sense to appear here in this book, and so it is important for me to acknowledge that Jonathan wrote the majority of this chapter.

we possess, that is to say, true and sound wisdom, consists of two parts: the knowledge of God and of ourselves."[2]

When thinking about our interactions with the dechurched, our need for a robust awareness of God cannot be understated. In fact, it is our God-awareness that grounds us and makes all other awarenesses truly possible. It propels us into the world with a bold dependence on him whom we know to already be intimately and sovereignly at work in the details of our lives and in the lives of those around us to bring about his purpose of redemption. Therefore, we can move out in confidence that God has already prepared good works beforehand that we should walk in them (Eph. 2:10), and that it is God who has interwoven our story with the stories of those who have left the church by intentionally placing us in the neighborhoods, workplaces, and relationships in which we find ourselves (Acts 17:26).

And as a result of this God-awareness, we can be confident that God has tasked us to wisely and gently implore people to "open the Gospels and hear [their] song once again"[3] and to "pay much closer attention to what we have heard, lest we drift away from it" (Heb. 2:1). Furthermore, we can also humbly endeavor to help "restore trust in the church" knowing that no one can "survive with the memory of a tune," and that "we need [the gospel] sung to us. We need it embodied and lived out in front of us."[4]

Therefore, this awareness of God in all of the deep-seated values in our society today helps us to "take [their][5] critiques more seriously, not less."[6]

---

2. John Calvin, *Institutes of the Christian Religion*, ed. F. L. Battles, trans. J. T. McNeill (Louisville: Westminster John Knox, 1960), 1:35.

3. Glen Scrivener, *The Air We Breathe: How We All Came to Believe in Freedom, Kindness, Progress, and Equality* (Charlotte, NC: Good Book Company, 2022), 194, Kindle.

4. Scrivener, 194.

5. Skeptics, critics, casually dechurched, and/or dechurched casualties alike.

6. Scrivener, 194.

Self-Awareness

We can have a healthy self-awareness only if we first have a profound awareness of God. If we aren't aware of God in our interactions with the dechurched, we might lack self-awareness by esteeming ourselves too much and thinking the rechurching of those around us depends solely on us. It doesn't. Lacking self-awareness will almost inevitably cause us to be like a pushy used-car salesman who is desperate to make a deal, which will most likely only push people *away from* rather than *toward* the gospel. Likewise, if we lack awareness of God, we may also lack self-awareness and actually esteem ourselves too little and thus ignore God's clear involvement of us in his purposes to "see to it that no one fails to obtain the grace of God" (Heb. 12:15).

Furthermore, Paul was quite clear concerning our self-awareness in evangelism in his letter to the Colossians. He instructed them to pray that he might *"make [the gospel] clear, which is how [he] ought to speak"* (Col. 4:4, emphasis added). A product of our self-awareness is our ability to *be clear* in our speech. This involves good listening and communication skills. Those who seek clarity in their speech will not assume that what they say will always be heard. Likewise, they will not assume that what they hear is always what was meant by the person speaking. As a result, self-aware persons will seek clarity in communication with others to remove any obstacle to the clarity of the gospel. This is especially important in a time in our culture when so many words and concepts have become emotionally supercharged.

Also important to our self-awareness is awareness of our own motives. It is critical that we assess *why* we are engaging with the dechurched. It cannot be for any reason apart from sincere affection for them that flows out of a genuine love of God. We should be careful to avoid motivations of spiritual pride, success, and praise from others. These kinds of motivations are unhealthy and run the risk of pushing people even further away. People aren't projects; they are human beings who bear the image of God.

Others-Awareness

The most natural fruit of God-awareness and self-awareness is others-awareness. This should not come as a surprise to us since this is nothing less than the great commandments given to us by Jesus: "You shall love the Lord your God with all your heart and with all your soul and with all your mind" and "You shall love your neighbor as yourself" (Matt. 22:37, 39). As a result of our awareness of God and of ourselves, our awareness of others is characterized by an understanding of what is important to those around us and of how they see the world. And others-awareness can only be gained in relationships. It means that we see others accurately and in context. This knowledge aligns our view of them more with God's, who sees them completely in context. We don't just want to persuade them more effectively; we want to meet their needs on every level (especially their deepest need) and to love them more as God does.[7]

This much is clear in Paul's instruction to the Colossian church. He said, "Walk in wisdom toward outsiders, making the best use of the time. Let your speech always be gracious, seasoned with salt, so that you may know how you ought to answer each person" (Col. 4:5–6). The only way one can really "walk in wisdom toward outsiders" and "let our speech be gracious and seasoned with salt" is if we have at least some relational capital with the person with whom we are speaking. This is because wisdom is the application of knowledge at the appropriate time and in the appropriate manner (hence our need to make the *best* use of the time). We can only know when and how to apply that knowledge if we have others-awareness.

Likewise, the graciousness and "saltiness" of our speech translate into our persuasion with others. And given the polarizing times in which we find ourselves, this is all the more important today. Again, this necessitates at least some relational knowledge

---

7. This insight comes from conversation with our friend Renee Jackson.

of the people with whom we are sharing the gospel. Seeing that the stumbling blocks of offense abound on both sides of the political spectrum in our current cultural climate, it is only wise to take some time to understand the people with whom we are speaking so as to best discern which topics to lean into and which topics to avoid in order to have a fruitful conversation about the gospel. We can only ultimately achieve this by assuming a humble and curious posture in relation to others that is marked by quickness to listen and slowness to speak (James 1:19).

Perhaps the best way to maintain this posture is by asking good questions. What typically makes questions "good" is that they are open-ended, not (too) leading, and genuinely curious:

> "How did you come to hold your conviction about _____?"
> "How do you feel like your belief in _____ is helping you in your everyday life?"
> "What do you think about your belief in comparison to other beliefs?"
> "What do you want from faith?"

Such questions can help us understand not only what someone believes but also how much relational "buying power" we have in our conversation in order to present gospel truth. This approach is what Joshua Chatraw emphasizes in his book *Telling a Better Story*. He underscores the "need for Christians to become better listeners who seek to understand the person they are speaking with before making appeals." He points out that "this enables us to meet people where they are and find points to affirm before finding points to challenge."[8] This is especially important with church casualties who often have legitimate reasons for leaving the church. By listening

---

8. Joshua Chatraw, *Telling a Better Story: How to Talk about God in a Skeptical Age* (Grand Rapids: Zondervan Reflective, 2020), 19–20, Kindle.

well, we may get the opportunity to remind our dechurched friends that it is actually on the basis of Christianity that we can "take [their] critiques *more* seriously, not less."[9] What if someone had done the hard work to move into Tammy's life either now or when the news broke of her daughter's assault (see chapter 5)?

Emotional Awareness

In a pandemic age when anxiety and depression abound due to loneliness and seclusion from relational connection, and when news sources and social media can so easily leave us in a state of heightened anxiety and angst, it is hard to understate the importance of our emotional awareness in how we relate to the dechurched. Of course, this isn't only important for us as we approach *others* with the gospel but also for us to be aware of first and foremost *in ourselves*. Our awareness of both ours and others' emotional states can have a big impact on how we deliver the gospel and how it is received.

For instance, in the midst of the prophet Isaiah's foretelling of God's messianic Servant, he describes him who would come, saying, "The Lord GOD has given Me the tongue of the learned, that I should know how to speak a word in season to him who is weary. He awakens Me morning by morning, He awakens My ear to hear as the learned" (Isa. 50:4 NKJV). This characteristic of the coming Christ sets the stage for how Jesus would exemplify an emotionally aware approach to sharing the gospel. He knew how to gauge the emotional temperature of those he encountered, and he knew how to "speak a word in season to him who is weary." In other words, he knew when and how to approach someone with gentleness so as to not break a "bruised reed" or snuff out a "smoldering wick" (Matt. 12:20).

---

9. Scrivener, *Air We Breathe*, 7, emphasis added.

Likewise, Jesus knew when his audience was emotionally antagonistic to his message, and as a result, he knew when not to "answer a fool according to his folly" (Prov. 26:4 NKJV). For instance, when the chief priests and elders approached Jesus to challenge his authority (Matt. 21:23–27), he knew their intention was not to humbly agree with his answer. So he asked them a question that he knew would bring the conversation to a stalemate and would allow him to decline to answer their question. This prevented an unnecessary emotional escalation that would have served only to harden the hearts of his questioners and further convince them of their irrational position.

We can learn how to notice the unspoken cues in our own hearts and in the hearts of others that give us insight into *how* to approach conversations with others. And as we learn to more accurately match "a word in season" to the emotional temperature of our hearers, we will see more doors of opportunity for the gospel and avoid unnecessarily antagonistic conversations that lead only to frustration and confusion. We think back to the way Sam did this so well, asking curious questions with Conor at the diner (see chapter 7).

Awareness of How Others Perceive Us

We would all be well served by the ability to jump into someone else's shoes to see how they experience us. If they experience us as being awkward, cringey, inappropriate, intense, uncomfortable, or any number of other unhelpful things, we would likely make important changes to our approach and engagement.

This is nothing less than what the apostle Paul sought to do when he became all things to all people so that by all means he might save some (1 Cor. 9:22). He was aware of and sought to remove any obstacle to the clarity of the gospel so that the offense of the cross might be the only offense his audience would experience.

This required self-awareness, others-awareness, and even awareness of how others might perceive him. Likewise, we should consider whether there might be ways in which we, like Paul, can lovingly choose to remove obstacles to the gospel for others.

If we fail to understand how others perceive us, we are likely to be ineffectual in reaching the dechurched. Though we are not ultimately responsible for how others perceive us, understanding the potential pressure points and pitfalls as they pertain to others' perceptions of us can be helpful when trying to communicate the gospel to them.

That said, as Rebecca McLaughlin points out, due to the complicated history of Christianity in this country, it's safe to say that many dechurched people we encounter may instinctively see Christians as "jerks."[10] As a result, it may be helpful to assume a posture that is quick to "confess both our own personal shortcomings and the failures of the church throughout history."[11] By doing so, we disarm those around us, and we help them perceive us as being safe rather than an angry threat.

One final distinction needs to be made here—the difference between transparency and vulnerability. Vulnerability is much deeper than transparency. When we are transparent with people, we let them see us for who we really are. When we are vulnerable, we allow people to speak into what they observed when we were transparent with them. Relational wisdom helps us know in what situations transparency and/or vulnerability are healthy. Ideally in deep friendship and community, we have a good degree of both transparency and vulnerability. Ideally we are also speaking of relationships in real life as opposed to generic online vulnerability, which is often problematic and sometimes illusory. Relationships of this kind are far more fertile for spiritual conversation that might otherwise be uncomfortable.

10. Rebecca McLaughlin, *The Secular Creed*, TGC Podcast, https://youtu.be/noM26VfBbBc.
11. Chatraw, *Telling a Better Story*, 19.

Cultural Awareness

Perhaps the most natural outgrowth of having a rich awareness of others is that of having a growing cultural awareness. Much like he addressed our need for others-awareness, Paul showed us our need for a broader cultural awareness when he instructed us to "walk in wisdom toward *outsiders*. . . . so that you may know how you ought to answer *each* person" (Col. 4:5–6, emphasis added). And the only way we can prepare to bring the gospel to bear on each person's particular situation is if we have at least a basic grasp on some of the nuances of our cultural moment. This is because individuals are always a reflection of their environments and cultural climates in one way or another, whether they are aware of this fact or not. The goal of cultural awareness is cultural humility. This type of humility is relationally disarming and helps to remove unnecessary barriers to the gospel that are cultural rather than spiritual.

Contextualization doesn't mean capitulation. For instance, we can and should hold to biblical sexual ethics, but we shouldn't make sexual ethics our only non-capitulating category. Yet cultural awareness and contextualization can help to show us *how* to engage difficult conversations. One of the largest studies of religious attitudes of LGBT persons found that "76% of LGBT people are open to returning to their religious community and their practices."[12] The same study found that 86 percent of LGBT persons were raised in a faith community, and more than "three-fourths were raised in *theologically conservative* religious communities."[13] Further, of those willing to return, only 8 percent of respondents indicated a desire for the faith community to change their theology as something that

---

12. Andrew Marin, *Us versus Us: The Untold Story of Religion and the LGBT Community* (Colorado Springs: NavPress, 2016), 65, Kindle.

13. Marin, 5, emphasis added. We are indebted here to Michael Horton's *Recovering Our Sanity: How the Fear of God Conquers the Fears That Divide Us* (Grand Rapids: Zondervan, 2022), for making us aware of Andrew Marin's book.

would influence them to return.[14] This is one of the most complicated conversations of our time. Hopefully, however, we can be encouraged that engaging with relational wisdom can help bridge even the most challenging conversations of our day.

Tim Keller helps readers confront cultural blindness in his book *How to Reach the West Again*, where he identifies seven basic cultural faith assumptions or narratives that characterize our culture and that "come to us now dozens of times a day—or even an hour—in ads, tweets, music, stories, opinion pieces, etc." We find his list both accurate and compelling:

- **IDENTITY:** "You have to be true to yourself."
- **FREEDOM:** "You should be free to live as you choose, as long as you don't hurt anyone."
- **HAPPINESS:** "You must do what makes you happiest. You can't sacrifice that for anyone."
- **SCIENCE:** "The only way to solve our problems is through objective science and facts."
- **MORALITY:** "Everyone has the right to decide what is right and wrong themselves."
- **JUSTICE:** "We are obligated to work for the freedom, rights, and good of everyone in the world."
- **HISTORY:** "History is bending toward social progress and away from religion."[15]

Regarding doing evangelism in our culture, Keller suggests that we need to "expose the main flaws in our culture's narratives, showing how they fit neither human nature nor our most profound intuitions about life—let alone its own moral ideals."[16] And the easiest

---

14. Marin, 65.

15. Timothy Keller, *How to Reach the West Again* (New York: Redeemer City to City, 2020), 40.

16. Keller, 18.

way to do this is by not just "answering questions" about the gospel, but instead by *questioning people's answers.*[17] This means we must not only be aware of the basic things people believe, but we must also gently and kindly demonstrate to our friends and family that their beliefs cannot deliver on their promises.

Practically speaking, this can look like asking a friend something like, "How do you know which part of you is your 'true self'?" Or "Who do you think should define what *hurt* means?" Or "Why do you think humans should have rights?" By asking questions like these, we invite people to be aware of their own presuppositions and faith assumptions and to examine their own cultural narratives, and we create space for a better narrative that only the gospel can provide.

To be even more practical, sometimes cultural awareness just means putting other cultures ahead of yours out of honor and respect. Recently the World Cup Final was scheduled for a Sunday morning. As the benediction at the end of our worship service was being pronounced, the game was tied up and headed to extra time. We have a number of non-Americans in our church, and many of them are Spanish speakers, many of them first generation. First, it was the loving thing to do to put the match on since nobody would have had time to catch it elsewhere and we respect that they still came to church even though the best World Cup Final of our lifetime was going on. Second, while we love the game, the clear right thing to do was pull up the Telemundo stream in Spanish. It was an extremely small thing that we could do, but it meant a lot to some people whom we care deeply about. Plus, if we are honest, the announcers are just better.

Sometimes cultural awareness involves big ideas and factors, and other times it just means actively thinking about others and finding ways to show deference, honor, and respect. A high level of cultural

---

17. Keller, 20, emphasis original.

awareness creates the cultural humility required for deeper connection through established trust.

Quiet, Calm Curiosity

What will it look like when we possess all six of these awarenesses? The simplest way it should look is quiet, calm curiosity.[18] When we are strong in our knowledge of God and our experience of him, our firm foundation should give us a calm and curious demeanor concerning others. Our goal is not to argue people into the kingdom of God. Certainly we can give well-reasoned explanations for our faith, but the key distinction is that we do so by persuading them with a better story.

We would all be wise to trade our defensiveness for curiosity. When some topic comes up about which we have strong opinions, feel the need to be right, or feel the need to justify ourselves, how we respond in those moments can invite transparency and vulnerability in the other person, or it can cause them to shut down. A genuinely curious posture helps others feel heard, understood, and safe.

The last decade has brought significant increases in situations that induce fear and anxiety—pandemic, polarizing national conversations, and the fracturing of numerous long-standing groups.[19] When we face stimuli or circumstances that are anxiety inducing, we tend to become emotionally dysregulated. In this state, the part of our brain where reasoning takes place (the prefrontal cortex) is largely bypassed and we end up reacting to those situations out of the part of our brain (the amygdala) that deals with fight, flight, or

---

18. I (Mike) am indebted here to conversations with Michael Keller and some of the broad ideas Mark Sayers speaks to in *A Non-Anxious Presence: How a Changing and Complex World Will Create a Remnant of Renewed Christian Leaders* (Chicago: Moody, 2022).

19. We have in mind everything from historic political alliances to denominational ties, to parachurch networks and local associations.

freeze.[20] When we live in high stress or anxiety circumstances, we can end up living in a constant cortisol state that can have all sorts of negative physiological consequences and also be very destructive relationally. If we hope to help other people, we must have our wits, reason, and faculties intact. This means we need an inner confidence in who we are, what we believe, and how we are to act. And when we possess that confidence, we can remain emotionally regulated and calm. For more persuadable persons, that calm will be contagious, but we shouldn't be surprised when others who are more prone to cycles of outrage become confused or frustrated when we don't mirror their cortisol state.

That calmness and curiosity should more frequently than not be quiet. Many Christians make the mistake of thinking they are influencing others only when they are talking. Good questions help people connect dots for themselves. When people connect dots for themselves, it is often far more powerful than if we just spell everything out because those people are experiencing self-discovery and internal ownership. To put it differently, how many times have you been in a conversation where the other person dominated it? Did you feel more relationally inclined to the parties involved afterward? Probably not. Are there things that people need to hear sometimes? Yes. Does the gospel require words? Yes. But possessing relational wisdom often means being quiet, calm, and curious in ways that are relationally disarming and help people own the connections they are making.

Through growing in competency in the respective awarenesses, we will invariably grow in our relational maturity. As a result, we will be filled with boldness and gentleness, with zeal and wisdom,

---

20. Rainbo Hultman, Stephen D. Mague, Qiang Li, et al., "Dysregulation of Prefrontal Cortex-Mediated Slow-Evolving Limbic Dynamics Drives Stress-Induced Emotional Pathology," *NIH National Library of Medicine* 91, no. 2 (July 20, 2016): 439–52, https://pubmed.ncbi .nlm.nih.gov/27346529/.

with curiosity and confidence to bring the gospel to bear on our culture.

Failure in even one or two of these competencies can give cover and excuses for people to leave the church. If people are going to leave the church or even the faith, let it be because of the offense of the gospel itself and not because we engaged them without relational wisdom.

Chapter 10

The Missed Generational Handoff

THE PASSING OF OUR FAITH FROM GENERATION TO GENERATION used to be almost assumed, but today the success rate of that handoff is plummeting. When I (Jim) was growing up in the '80s and '90s, it was common to be in church on Sunday and look around and see three and even four generations of families sitting together in the same pews each week. What was common just thirty years ago is a novelty in many churches today. Since the 1990s, the faith of younger generations has plummeted and is only accelerating downward.

Scripture could not be clearer in our responsibility to pass our faith on to the next generation. As far back as Moses, God's people have been commanded to love God and pass on this love:

> Hear, O Israel: The LORD our God, the LORD is one. You shall love the LORD your God with all your heart and with all your soul and with all your might. And these words that I command you today shall be on your heart. You shall teach them diligently to your children, and shall talk of them when you sit in your house, and

when you walk by the way, and when you lie down, and when you rise. You shall bind them as a sign on your hand, and they shall be as frontlets between your eyes. You shall write them on the doorposts of your house and on your gates. (Deut. 6:4–9)

Figure 10.1. Share Believing in God without a Doubt

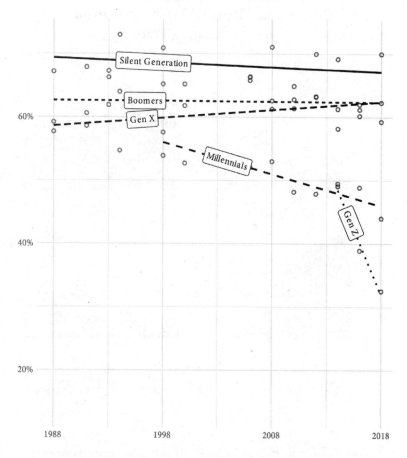

Ryan Burge, "'OK Millennial': Don't Blame the Boomers for Decline of Religion in America," Religion News Service, August 30, 2021, https://religionnews.com/2021/08/30/ok-millennial-dont-blame-the-boomers-for-decline-of-religion-in-america/.

It is significant that in our study when we asked survey participants in what period of their life they were most religious, the period of highest religious interest was from ages 0–18 and the period of lowest religious interest was ages 18–25. That alone highlights the rough transition as young adults leave their parents' homes and start their own lives.

Figure 10.2. Most Difficult Transition in Maintaining Faith

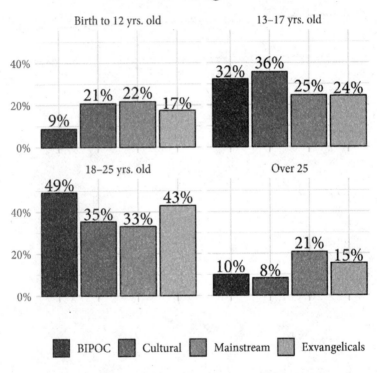

last few decades. In 1972 just 5 percent of adults in the United States said they had no religious affiliation. Twenty years later, that had gone up just two percentage points. But from that point forward, the nones continued to creep up a percentage point or two every year. By 2021 the share of Americans who were nones was about 30 percent.

What has lagged much further behind is the percentage of people who say they were raised without religion. Among those born in the 1950s, just 4 percent said their household had no religious influence. Among those born in the 1990s, that share had risen to only 14 percent. However, among the youngest Americans, a third of them say they have no religion by the time they hit their twenty-fifth birthday.

Among the nones, half of the religious disaffiliation is caused by young people raised in nonreligious households, while the other half is teens and college-age students leaving religion behind as they move into their late twenties. But a college education is not necessarily pushing people out of church; the opposite may be true.

Among 18- to 22-year-olds who are going to college, just 27 percent describe their religion as "nothing in particular." That number is 37 percent among those who are not attending college. The share of atheists and agnostics is the same between college- and non-college-attending young people, as well. Thus, there's little evidence in the data that education is driving secularization. Other forces are at play that social science has not yet been fully able to determine.

We examined the animating concerns of those who dechurched from evangelical churches between the ages of 13 and 17 and between the ages of 18 and 25. It is worth mentioning that those who dechurched from mainline churches and Roman Catholic churches had a much higher rate of dechurching in these stages, with the most significant being right after high school.

The three stages when it is most difficult to hold on to the faith and when the generational handoff is most often missed are the high school years, the four years after high school (usually in college), and the early years of becoming established in a new career or vocation. In this chapter, we created fictional characters based on the dechurching data to illustrate these three stages.

Transition 1:
Lucy in High School

First, we want to tell you about Lucy. She is a seventeen-year-old Latino girl living in Nashville with her parents. She grew up attending a nondenominational church but never felt like she fit in. In hopes of keeping their youth engaged, this church had a separate worship service for all youth through middle school. When she got to high school, she tried to plug into the high school youth but found it difficult to make friends her ninth-grade year. Lucy was a particularly gifted athlete, and travel soccer began to eat up many of her Sundays, which made it even more difficult to develop meaningful relationships.

When Lucy was in tenth grade, her parents stopped attending church. They had no problem with the church, but they could see that Lucy's primary community was at her school, particularly on her travel soccer team. Lucy got her driver's license that year and had her first serious relationship with a boy from school named Adam. He was a nice boy but not a Christian. He was an agnostic who had significant disagreements with the teachings of the Bible and the role of the church. Lucy had never really doubted God but began to privately question. She didn't admit this to Adam or her parents. She wanted to talk to someone, but she didn't feel like she could open up to her parents about her doubts.

This was also the year in which Lucy became sexually active for the first time. She was torn between a real love for Adam and some guilt because she had grown up hearing that she should wait until marriage to have sex. This wasn't a message she had heard recently, as church attendance was extremely sparse these days. Actually, the only time her family went was when there was no soccer and there was a specific reason like Christmas Eve or Easter.

On one of these occasions, Lucy found herself in church desiring answers and guidance but unsure of where to get them. The messages she heard seemed shallow given the deeper questions she was wrestling with about God and her sexual ethic. She was worried that if she opened up to other students in the youth group, she would be judged for her decisions, but she didn't have relationships with any older Christians, so she just kept quiet. She didn't feel safe admitting to anyone in the church that she doubted God and was sleeping with her boyfriend.

The next year was pivotal for Lucy. In eleventh grade, she decided to stop going to church unless her parents wanted to take her, which only happened on special days like Christmas Eve, Easter, and maybe Mother's Day. Lucy and Adam broke up, but she was a starter now on her high school soccer team and devoted her time to that. She made good grades, and from her perspective, her future looked bright.

Lucy decided she did believe in God, but he felt far off. She believed the church was a good institution, but it felt mostly irrelevant to her life. She still prayed to Jesus on occasion, but she was open to other ways to God as well. Lucy went on to a nearby university after high school, where she played soccer her freshman year, but she gave it up after that. She never attended church while in college but was open to it if it was important to her future husband.

What could have changed Lucy's course? No one can say for sure, but if you ask her, she would say that if her parents had prioritized church, that would have made a real difference. If her parents felt more approachable, she would have been able to talk to them about her doubts. She would also say that she wishes the church she attended would have addressed the issues she was dealing with more and that she would have liked more access to older believers she could have talked to.

Lucy Explained

Twenty-eight percent of the dechurched evangelicals surveyed said this was the stage of life when it was most difficult to maintain their faith. As to why, 12 percent cited a struggle to fit in or belong, 10 percent cited a lack of people their age to connect with, 9 percent cited some bad experiences in the church, and another 9 percent said life just got busy or they had other priorities.

Lucy was a product of the 13 percent of dechurched evangelicals in our survey whose parents stopped bringing them to church because life got busy. The church was not helpful to her because she believed the Bible was not taught clearly or often enough (23%) and that God seemed missing from her experience (20%). She, along with 17 percent of those who dechurched from an evangelical church at a young age felt like the church would judge her because of her sexual activity.[1] Sadly, many who dechurch between the ages of 15 and 25 don't feel comfortable admitting doubts (23%) or asking their most pressing questions in the church (36%).[2]

---

1. "Six Reasons Young Christians Leave Church," Barna, September 27, 2011, https://www.barna.com/research/six-reasons-young-christians-leave-church/.
2. "Six Reasons Young Christians Leave Church."

Figure 10.3. What Made the Transition from Teen to Young Adult Difficult?

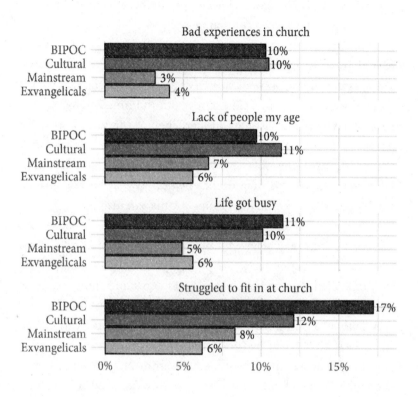

Bad experiences in church

- BIPOC — 10%
- Cultural — 10%
- Mainstream — 3%
- Exvangelicals — 4%

Lack of people my age

- BIPOC — 10%
- Cultural — 11%
- Mainstream — 7%
- Exvangelicals — 6%

Life got busy

- BIPOC — 11%
- Cultural — 10%
- Mainstream — 5%
- Exvangelicals — 6%

Struggled to fit in at church

- BIPOC — 17%
- Cultural — 12%
- Mainstream — 8%
- Exvangelicals — 6%

0%   5%   10%   15%

Transition 2: Drew in College

Drew went to a conservative Christian high school in Charlotte, North Carolina, and his parents faithfully took him to a Presbyterian (PCA) church. Drew's parents were very controlling about what he watched and who he hung out with. Drew would say his parents did not listen well and became defensive when he would ask questions about their worldview and argumentative when he disagreed.

He perceived his parents to have intolerant views about race and a hypocritical attitude when it came to loving others. While they held traditional Christian views on gender, his father was harsh and condescending in the way he communicated those views.

For Drew church was boring, but he understood it was just part of growing up in that household. After graduating high school, Drew attended the University of Georgia where he could make his own decisions for the first time. Drew almost immediately began to make what his parents would consider rebellious and self-destructive decisions. While Drew maintained good grades, partying and sex became the things he looked forward to the most. He had never been allowed to choose his own friends before now, as he was given a small pool of "acceptable friendships" by his parents.

Drew was interested in joining a fraternity, but his parents would not pay for it as they believed it would have negative effects on his Christian life. They encouraged him to get involved in a campus ministry or student government. He had no interest in joining a campus ministry because he realized that his faith had really just been his parents' faith all along, and he no longer held that same faith. While he still believed in God, he had no desire to pursue God or attend a campus ministry or church. As for student government, he saw his parents' overemphasis on the culture war and honestly wondered if they cared more about politics or Jesus. His dad had been a leader in his church back home, and Drew saw him most passionate when talking about the Republican Party or passing out voter guides in church on Sunday.

During Drew's sophomore year, his sister confided in him that she was gay. She wasn't sure what to do with these desires but knew she could not talk to their parents about them. She also did not think her parents, especially her father, would listen. She had heard his tirades over the years about gay marriage and had seen his anger when this topic came up. Drew loved his sister and wanted to be supportive, but this also created another justification in him to embrace a sexual ethic other than his parents' views, which he considered stifling and archaic. In fact, he started to realize his Christian upbringing was largely stifling, fear-based, and risk-averse. He was truly enjoying doing the things he had grown up seeing his church demonize.

Drew began to wonder what else his parents might be wrong about. Throughout his sophomore and junior years, he began to notice that his parents believed they had all the answers. They had little room for gray issues, and they seemed to be out of touch with the scientific world he was learning about in college. His professors mocked the creation views he had been raised to assume. Drew still believed in a creator but that there were many ways to relate to him outside of the teachings he grew up on from the Bible. From this point on, Drew had two aims he wanted to pursue in life: money and sex.

During Drew's senior year, he decided to stay in North Georgia after school and use his business degree to make money, but he liked his new, free Sunday mornings and had no desire to give them up to feel guilty about the life he was living. He was a fiscal conservative, but his views on sexuality, alcohol, and church would be far to the left of his upbringing. He saw little the church could offer him that his functional gods of wealth and women could not. Drew was glad to be free from his Christian upbringing but would still attend church with his parents when visiting home and on holidays.

Drew Explained

Like 13 percent of dechurched evangelicals in our survey and 9 percent of that group who dechurched in this season, Drew didn't feel like his faith was his own and that it was really borrowed from his parents. Drew struggled to fit in with his church upbringing (like 13 percent of those in our study who dechurched from evangelical churches during this transitional time of life) because instead of equipping him to live in the world, they primarily tried to protect him from the world. He wanted to explore his sexuality in ways that were not acceptable to his church or family (5%), and his sister's acknowledgment of her own struggle pushed him to pursue his own sexual ethic.

A huge number of dechurched evangelicals (30%) said that if their parents had just embodied love, joy, gentleness, and kindness more or listened to them more (30%), they might not have left the church. In addition to that, they wished their parents had charitably engaged with other viewpoints (17%) instead of just denigrating them. Drew's life got busy after college, and his new priorities on Sunday morning and Saturday night took him away from church (12%), but he didn't miss church because of the bad experiences he had there (11%). He now enjoys the benefits of his surplus finances (10%) and isn't looking back.

It's worth noting that those who are involved in a campus ministry during their college years are more than three times more likely to stay in church after college. Now, there is certainly some selection bias here, as those who opt in to a campus ministry are already more likely to stay in church after college, but even so, this point cannot be glossed over. The work campus ministers are doing is vital and must be supported.

Figure 10.4. Religious Involvement during College Years among Evangelicals

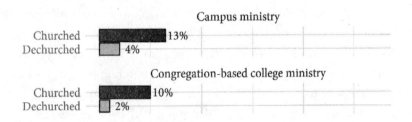

Figure 10.4 Continued

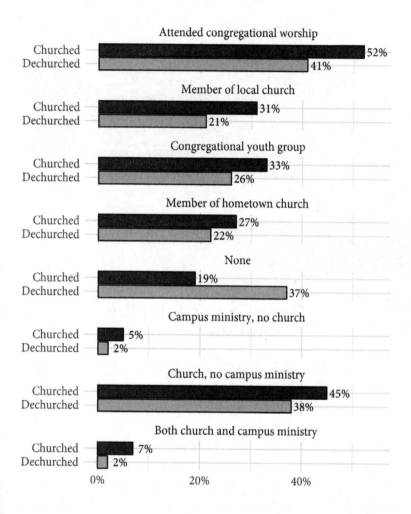

As we mentioned in chapter 2, college itself is not the boogeyman. Drew didn't have what he needed before he left. College didn't lead him astray; it just created new freedom that he didn't have at home to explore what he considered to be deficiencies in the faith he grew up in.

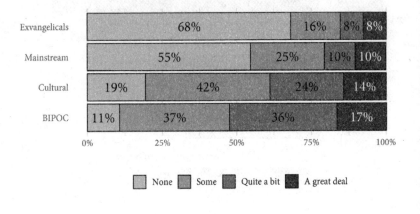

Figure 10.5. How Big of an Influence
Were Your Parents When It Comes to
No Longer Attending Church?

Transition 3: John the Young Professional

John grew up attending a Baptist church with his parents in Tampa, Florida. He attended the University of Florida, where he periodically went to a campus ministry his first two years but stopped after that. John battled depression throughout college and did not find his faith to have any helpful answers to find a way out of it. During his sophomore and junior years, he attended church about once a month at the request of his girlfriend, but they broke up early into his senior year. John graduated, moved back to Tampa, and took a job in the medical sales industry.

Initially, John went to church with his parents but realized he was only doing it for them and the outside possibility of meeting a girl there. John was invited to happy hours after work and began to connect with other young professionals in the same stage of life as him. John had his own money for the first time and would go to nice parties on the weekends where he made more friends. John's passions were fishing and golf, and he had no trouble finding friends with the same interests. He had the money, time, and connections to go fishing offshore and even made some trips to the Bahamas. At the age of twenty-five, John got a great promotion, and he joined a local golf club.

For John, life seemed to be going great. But his depression never left him. He saw a counselor, which seemed to help, but in his view, the church had nothing to offer him. His parents often asked if he was going to any kind of church, but he would deflect by saying he was just too busy. It wasn't a lie. John was often traveling on the weekend, but if he was in town on Sunday, he was usually on the golf course, maybe nursing a hangover. John's career was the most important thing to him now.

One Sunday morning after a round of golf, John was eating lunch with friends at the clubhouse when he met Angela through a mutual friend. Angela was a beautiful, young real estate broker from Orlando in her mid-twenties. They hit it off, and in just a few months they were spending most of their evenings and weekends together. Angela had not grown up going to church. She wasn't against the church but didn't know much about it or see its relevance. Six months after meeting, they made the decision to move in together.

John's parents weren't thrilled about them living together, but they were glad he seemed happy. Today John rarely thinks about church anymore, but he does think about God. He prays when things seem tough, and he is thankful for the blessings he sees. When he prays, he ends his prayers "in Jesus' name." If you press him, he would affirm the Trinity and the resurrection, but he isn't sure about the exclusivity of Jesus or the reliability of the Bible. John sometimes wonders if he will return to church when he has children one day. It could be a tough sell to Angela if they do get married, but John doesn't want to rock the boat on that topic with her. For now, John is dechurched.

John Explained

John, along with more than 60 percent of dechurched evangelicals in our survey, is still orthodox if you press him on the most important doctrines of the faith and would come back to church if it was a priority for Angela (18%). John still feels a void in his life and believes that God can fill it, but he doesn't see church as the answer, because when he was growing up, his church didn't have helpful categories for how to deal with his depression. Instead of suggesting a professional therapist, his parents' answer was to read his Bible more.

John found his new community through his professional relationships (like 9 percent of young professionals in our study who dechurched from evangelicalism) but believes he will return to church one day (51%)—maybe after he has kids.

Young People Need Churches

We could tell many other stories. We could tell the story of Antonio and the 17 percent of BIPOC Christians who struggle to fit in at church. We could tell the story of Tracy who grew up in a mainline church and never heard the gospel clearly in all her years at church. But we chose these three stories because they encompass those of millions of young people in the hardest season of life to maintain faith.

We have used the imagery of passing the baton, but that imagery falls short of the goal of a faith family. Maybe a better image is that of three generations of a family building a house. Instead of a one-second baton pass, we strive to work together over the course of decades to build and be a part of something beautiful. Neither Lucy, Drew, nor John had that experience. The older generations seem to assume that if they do the same things their parents did, their children will, as they did, make the church a priority in their lives.

The truth is that their children and grandchildren are growing up in a completely different world than they did. America of the 1960s, '70s, and '80s encouraged people to be a part of a church in a way that it no longer does. In addition, the growth of extracurricular activities and sports demanding Sunday morning attendance have created an additional pull away from church involvement. Young people today can explore literally any worldview or ethic they want in complete privacy on their devices. They need parents who are safe spaces where they can process hard questions. They need parents who are willing to say, "I don't know," but who are also willing to walk with them to find those answers.

Young people need churches that are more serious about securing souls than filling up seats. They need pastors who help them to follow Jesus as we Christians live as exiles in this world instead of putting our hope in politicians to make our culture the way it once was. Young people need real answers to their questions—answers that are found in the Bible and secured in the gospel, and that change lives through the power of the Holy Spirit.

Raising up the next generation in the faith takes the whole church working and praying together to build something beautiful for the next generation instead of a few working to create a Sunday morning experience. It is possible. It will take men and women embodying the fruit of the Spirit, determined to pray and to listen. It will take a community that makes it okay not to be okay because we all are works in progress moving toward glory by the grace of Jesus.

Chapter 11

Messages for the Dechurched

WHEN I (JIM) WAS GROWING UP IN ORLANDO, MOST OF THE PEOPLE I knew were churchgoers. Then, when I was twenty-one years old, I asked a guy where he went to church. His reply was, "I don't." That seemed extremely odd to me—so much so that it has been ingrained in my mind to this day. Now most of the people I'm around used to go to church but no longer do. Some are dechurched casualties, and many more have casually dechurched. This whole book came from a desire to get better at engaging that context. So, how do we engage? *Helpfully.* That is the operative word.

Acts 17 gives us the account of Paul at the Areopagus, the hill of the Greek god Ares, in Athens, a main location for pagan worship. There Paul provided a great example of engagement that is both missional and confessional. Paul's model was to comprehend, commend, and then critique.[1] Whatever worldview we may interact with, chances are it will seem tame compared to what Paul engaged

---

1. This rubric is something I have heard from multiple sources.

in Athens. Paul first comprehended the worldview with which he wanted to engage. Before he said a word, he listened and he studied. Similarly, the dechurched hold unique worldviews that we must understand before we can effectively engage.

Second, Paul commended these people. He praised something about the worship of these Greek pagans! Paul had many reasons to denounce their false worship, but that is not where he started. He said, "Men of Athens, I perceive that in every way you are very religious" (Acts 17:22). Paul was not endorsing their false worship; he was simply commending their belief that there was something worthy of worship that they hadn't yet seen. He affirmed that they were right to worship but not that their worship was right. As we will soon see, our dechurched friends can and should be commended as well.

We would go so far as to say that if you can't commend some aspect of the dechurched person's worldview, you haven't comprehended it yet, and any critique will not be helpful. God has designed this world in such a way that a worldview that is 100 percent devoid of truth will never get off the ground. Satan perverts and misapplies truth, but he can never be rid of it completely. The process of commending the beliefs and practices of other worldviews also helps to ensure that our own hearts are in the right place. If you can't commend a different worldview, you may have a hard heart in need of repentance before you can help.

Then we arrive at the critique. Paul didn't immediately confront the pagan worldview. He did not accommodate it or syncretize it into his faith. He pointed these Greeks to Jesus in a way that would be heard. He knew they had an altar to an unknown god, and he said, "For as I passed along and observed the objects of your worship, I found also an altar with this inscription, 'To the unknown god.' What therefore you worship as unknown, this I proclaim to you" (Acts 17:23). He then preached the gospel. Paul applied this same method to Jewish cultures around the Roman Empire. In the words of Joshua Chatraw, "This enables us to meet people where they are and find points to affirm before finding points to challenge."[2]

Let's now apply Paul's method to the dechurched by identifying six messages they need to hear from the church based on some of the top reasons people have left the church. In this chapter, we are using data from phase 2, which zeros in on those who have dechurched from every tradition.

Figure 11.1. Reasons for Dechurching

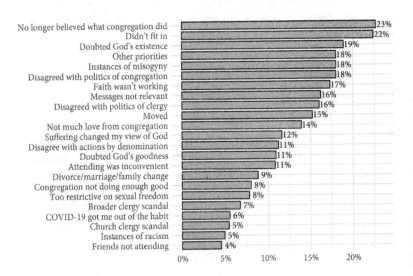

The Political Issue: The Gospel Comes with an Ethic
===

We know that many Americans have left the church because of political disagreements. They haven't just left *a* church; they have

---

2. Joshua Chatraw, *Telling a Better Story: How to Talk about God in a Skeptical Age* (Grand Rapids: Zondervan Reflective, 2020), 19, Kindle.

left *the* church. Eighteen percent left because of political disagreements with the congregation. Sixteen percent left because of political
disagreements with the clergy. Some do it amicably, saying things
like, "I don't agree with the politics of my pastor, and rather than be
a thorn in his side, I'd rather just not go." Others leave, saying things
like, "The church seemed to care more about issues of race and politics than the gospel."

We should be willing to sit and hear these concerns, for we won't
truly comprehend them until we can, at some level, feel them. We
currently live in a highly polarized time, and it should not surprise us
that these polarizations are also felt inside the church.

What can we commend when we engage these people? We can
say, "We share your concerns." Dechurching is happening among
both the secular left and the secular right, and if either side is more
passionate about the politics of our country than about the gospel of
Jesus Christ, something is wrong. In our own context, we have had
passionate debates in our leadership as to whether it is appropriate to
pass out right-wing voter guides in November, *and* we have experienced fallout from the left for not speaking out more on the moral
failings of our leaders or done more to support issues like reparations
and the conditions that make men and women more likely to find
themselves facing the question of abortion.

The critique, though, is that there is no such thing as a
Christianity with no political implications. Those on the political
right who tell pastors to stay out of politics on issues of race and justice tend to be the most vocal on pro-life issues, which are extremely
political. The gospel comes with an ethic that will always overlap
with our national political conversation. The question is which takes
priority in our churches.

We must put primary issues in the primary spot and secondary
and tertiary issues in their proper places. Certainly, the core historic Christian theological doctrines are primary. These include the
divinity of Jesus, his atonement for our sin, his resurrection, and

our sure hope of an eternity with God free from sin if we place our faith in him. There are primary implications of our doctrine that we should agree on as well. If we are all made in the image of God, then we agree that racism is bad and the unborn should be protected. How exactly we move forward, though, on these fronts can be complicated. The *how* is the application of wisdom and therefore becomes a secondary issue.

Those who have dechurched because of politics should first ask themselves if they have the primary and secondary in their proper places. Did they possibly leave too hastily? Have the secondary issues become primary for them? Or did they rightly see that the church and clergy were guilty of the misalignment of the gospel ethic? If that is the case, the second message might be helpful.

The Hurt Issue: You Don't Have to Return to What You Left

We know that 22 percent of the dechurched in our survey left the church because they felt like they didn't fit in, and 14 percent left because they felt unloved by their congregation. But hearing a statistic is not the same as comprehending a person's story. I (Jim) recently heard a friend say, "I attended a large church in town for over a decade and had to stop attending due to major health issues. Not one person in that church seemed to notice that I was gone, and no one ever called to check on me. I have stopped going to church altogether and will never go back to that church." Another friend lamented to me, "I got a look under the hood, and I don't trust what I saw. In that church, I existed to serve the leadership. They clearly had no interest in serving the congregation."

What can we commend here? We can commend their desire to fit in and be loved. These are not unreasonable desires or expectations. Paul's main plea to the Corinthian church was to love one another. Jesus said the world will know something about the Father through the unity of the church (John 17:23).

We might even commend their departure from that church. Maybe it was a good decision! A church should know its people. A church should know enough to pray for and visit the sick in its midst. A church should understand that its leadership exists to serve and not be served. These are not unreasonable values, and maybe the best way we can commend people who left for these reasons is to simply say that we would have left that church too.

Sometimes, though, people leave with even more significant hurt or trauma that requires even more listening to comprehend. Nine percent of those who have left the church cite misogyny as the reason for their departure. The fact that many of the dechurched perceive the church to be patriarchal, unhelpfully hierarchical, and oppressive to women is a reality with which we must engage. It's easy to read those words, especially if you are in church leadership, and be dismissive or defensive. We don't want to be harsh, but if you feel resistance to that statistic rising up inside of you, you may still have some work to do in comprehending the problem.

Again, let's hear the story and not just the statistics. Mars Hill Church, pastored by Mark Driscoll, was one of the most influential churches in the world during the early part of this century, until it came crashing down almost overnight. Here is what Mark taught in 2001: "You may be able to show me a family where the kids are well loved and the wife works full-time and everything is great, and I will show you a thousand that are not. And I will tell you that the majority should speak loudly. And in this church that's the way it's going to be. I won't lie to you. Because I am responsible for the families. And I am responsible for the conditions of the homes."[3]

Looking back, one of the pastors, Tim Smith, recalled, "If a

---

3. Mike Cosper, "The Things We Do to Women," *Christianity Today*, July 26, 2021, https://www.christianitytoday.com/ct/podcasts/rise-and-fall-of-mars-hill/mars-hill-mark-driscoll-podcast-things-we-do-women.html.

woman was interested in anything outside the home, the advice and the challenge to the men was to lead your wife better, and the advice to the women was to get married if they weren't, and if they were, to have another kid. Because then they wouldn't have time for as many other ambitions. At multiple points, particularly early on in the church, it was seen as a disqualification, especially in the office of elder, if the woman worked outside the home."[4]

In the words of one woman in that church, "I think the problem is that unfortunately, [biblical masculinity] gets couched with feminists, and women's rights and women in the workplace and any kind of empowerment of women outside the home was then unfortunately problematized."[5]

We have not comprehended until we have heard the stories. How, then, might we commend the people who have left a church because of misogyny? We can start by affirming that God did not give us a church that should promote misogyny or inequality in any way. The Bible holds a higher view of women than its surrounding culture. This was true in ancient Israel and even more so in the Roman Empire when Paul wrote, "There is neither Jew nor Greek, there is neither slave nor free, there is *no male and female*, for you are all one in Christ Jesus" (Gal. 3:28, emphasis added). In a day when women were regarded as property who could be divorced for almost any reason, Paul declared that they were of equal value to their male counterparts. This was nothing short of shocking to Paul's audience and still speaks loudly to us today.

Even churches that restrict the office of elder to men have a biblical duty to lift women up by developing their gifts and building them up in every way possible. Sometimes there is no greater way to commend someone in this situation than to say, "You were right to leave. I would have left that church too."

---

4. Cosper.
5. Cosper.

What, then, is the critique? You don't have to return to what you left! You should return to *a* church, but it doesn't have to be nor should it be *that* church. While there is no such thing as a perfect church, many churches value knowing, serving, and loving their people. There are churches that strive to show men and women equal honor and churches that prayerfully work hard to more accurately reflect biblical values in their congregation. And maybe your story will have something important to contribute to that imperfect but striving church.

The Streaming Issue: "Online Worship" Is Not the Gathering

According to 2022 Pew research, 21 percent of practicing Christians are only worshiping online.[6] Our own research shows that percentage as even higher, at around a third of practicing Christians. Figure 11.1 at the start of this chapter shows a much smaller percentage, but those are the people who dechurched *because* online accessibility came about. A much larger percentage have already dechurched but still only worship online now that it has come available.

This group of online worshipers has grown significantly through COVID-19, as nearly every church pivoted to make some kind of online experience available during quarantine. Our own church made the same pivot, and we are thankful for technology that allowed us to remain connected in some way during that unique pandemic period. We should commend the desire of individuals to pursue Christian teachings and practices during the week or when issues like health prevent them from attending.

---

6. Justin Nortey, "More Houses of Worship Are Returning to Normal Operations, but In-Person Attendance Is Unchanged Since Fall," Pew Research Center, March 22, 2022, https://www.pewresearch.org/fact-tank/2022/03/22/more-houses-of-worship-are-returning-to-normal-operations-but-in-person-attendance-is-unchanged-since-fall/.

Even though this chapter is primarily addressing messages to the dechurched, on this issue, we must also address the church. We commend the desire of churches to make services even more accessible to the masses and to use technology as a way of moving people from their homes and cars into physical, on-location worship with other Christians. Technology as a vehicle to that end instead of a replacement for real pastors, on-site Communion, corporate prayer, and discipleship can be a real blessing to the kingdom.

I (Jim) heard a story recently about a large church that has launched a meta-worship experience. At first, I rolled my eyes at the idea. But they have church staff in that meta world poking people to see if they can encourage them to meet with a real person and one day worship on location. There was one man in the meta-worship who would never respond, but eventually he created a virtual sparkler in his hand and with it wrote the word *China*. This man had no safe access to Bible teaching, but this new technology was not yet monitored by the Chinese government and was safe for him to step into and worship. This blew all my categories for meta-worship and helped me to appreciate how technology can be innovatively used to bring the gospel where it is not.

Having said that, we want to be clear that those who are able to worship in person but choose not to must be called what they are: dechurched. As I (Jim) wrote with Skyler Flowers in May 2021,

> Worshiping as a church is an embodied experience, in both its individual and communal dimensions. The Bible is clear that gathering is essential for the life of the church. In Matthew 18:17–20, in the context of Jesus speaking about the church, he makes his beloved promise: "where two or three are gathered in my name, there am I among them." Paul admonishes Christians to celebrate the Lord's Supper when they have come together (1 Cor. 11:33). The author of Hebrews tells us to not neglect meeting together (Heb. 10:25).

We are not simply minds that passively take in the prayers, teaching, and worship of a worship service. Rather, as those created body and mind after the image of God, we must experience what is sung, prayed, taught, and tasted in worshiping God with our whole selves. Our voices lift up together in corporate confession in song. Our hearts bow in corporate submission in prayer. Our bodies partake in a corporate meal in the Lord's Supper. We are corporately commissioned with a blessing from the Lord in benediction. In many traditions, the sermon is the pinnacle of this corporate gathering, through which God addresses his people.

These are actions of a covenant people in a covenant assembly worshiping the covenant God. Trying to accomplish these things by yourself through a device pales in comparison to the real thing. A faint hint of that experience can be felt in a livestream, but at its best, livestreaming is the spiritual equivalent of a deployed soldier having a Zoom relationship with his wife: necessary, but nothing you'd want to get used to.[7]

We have enough data now to see that streaming fuels consumeristic church, enables laziness, and fools people into thinking they're being nourished and built up. Online church is the CliffsNotes of worship. It's a cheap substitute.

When I (Jim) lived overseas, every so often I would go onto a US military base. Immediately when you pass the gates, you are on US soil. All the signs are in English, the fashion is American, and you begin to see great dining establishments like Pizza Hut and Burger King. You pay in American dollars, and you see glimpses of home in things like free refills, American architecture, and police cars that make the "correct" siren sound. When on base, we were a small group of very different people far from home but, in a way, home at the same time.

7. Jim Davis and Skyler Flowers, "Why Our Church Will Unplug from Streaming," TGC, May 27, 2021, https://www.thegospelcoalition.org/article/why-church-will-unplug/.

That is what the Sunday gathering is for us. We come together as a diverse group of people feeling acutely that we are not home—a people who, in some mysterious way, leave the world we live in to worship the King of our new kingdom. And, for a moment, even if we aren't truly there, we can taste the home we long for. Our Sunday gathering has a centering effect on us, and to the degree we make the gathering a priority in our lives, we will taste our true home and flourish as citizens of heaven on earth.

It is also important that we give the gift of corporate worship to our children. It has a major impact in shaping their worldview. If we don't prioritize gathered worship in our lives, why would our children do so later in life? What kind of effect will that have on our grandchildren? The gathered worship of God's people is supernaturally powerful, and it is one of the greatest gifts we can give our children, so we must make it a priority in their lives.

In worship we are reminded that we are God's children, his beloved. That we are a part of a spiritual family that will never be broken. That we were wayward, but the Father found us. We are wandering, but the Father will bring us home. Every Sunday in every church across this globe, our minds and hearts are reminded of the most important things in life. Christians are made for active participation in the local church.

RYAN BURGE: The COVID-19 pandemic brought a cascade of difficult decisions for churches to make in trying to navigate government mandates, public health concerns, and the spiritual and emotional needs of their members. The Pew Research Center fielded a poll in the first week of March 2021 when the number of COVID-19 cases was still uncomfortably high, and the responses indicate that the vast majority of churches had changed the way they conducted services due to these restrictions. Just 12 percent of monthly church attenders said their church was open without any restrictions, while 18 percent said their church was not meeting at all for in-person worship. The remainder said they were meeting in person but with restrictions like masking, limited attendance, and social distancing.

As a way to still allow people to gather, many churches pivoted to online worship services that people could enjoy from the comfort of their home. Eighty-two percent of respondents indicated that this was something their current house of worship was doing because of the pandemic's shutdowns. But as American society emerges on the other side of COVID-19, many churches are asking themselves if they should continue to stream online in conjunction with face-to-face worship services. The data tells an interesting story.

Among those who reported watching a worship service online in the prior month, 30 percent also said they had attended church in person during the previous four weeks. That means most people who were watching a religious service online did not step foot in a church. Online church was their only connection to their congregation. However, among those who reported still attending church in person, 57 percent indicated that they were watching services online, as well. For many, online worship became a supplement to their face-to-face church attendance.

Thus, online worship was utilized both by people who couldn't go to church and by those who were still attending faithfully in person. Choosing to eliminate that option or scale it back significantly is not an easy decision. Balancing a desire to return to normal operations with the possibility of extending the gospel to those who are unwilling or unable to come to church is something every leadership team has to consider.

The Abuse Issue:
Blessed Are the Little Ones

In 2004 a report commissioned by the Roman Catholic Church surfaced four thousand Roman Catholic priests over the past fifty years who had allegations of sexual abuse against them involving more than ten thousand children.[8] In a bombshell May 2022 report, an independent investigation claimed the leadership of the Southern Baptist Convention (SBC) mishandled credible allegations of sexual abuse, intimidated victims and their advocates, and resisted attempts at reform over the past two decades.[9] In my (Jim's) early years of pastoring, I was made aware of sexual abuse allegations involving a minor and immediately took the issue to the police. To my shock, over the years I've learned of many situations where church leaders failed to report in similar circumstances.

How could those with the most power and influence so seriously harm those who have the least? How could others ignore or even cover up the abuse, allowing the perpetrators to go on to harm other children? Seven percent of those studied in phase 2 dechurched because of broader clergy scandal, and 5 percent did because of clergy scandal in their church. When we focused only on dechurched evangelicals, those percentages both rose to 12 percent. While these scandals are not limited to abuse of women and children in the church, they do represent an abuse of the office.

To those who have dechurched over this issue, we must say in the strongest way that the people involved in this unchristian

---

8. The John Jay College of Criminal Justice, "The Nature and Scope of Sexual Abuse of Minors by Catholic Priests and Deacons in the United States 1950–2002," US Conference of Catholic Bishops, February 2004, https://www.usccb.org/sites/default/files/issues-and-action/child-and-youth-protection/upload/The-Nature-and-Scope-of-Sexual-Abuse-of-Minors-by-Catholic-Priests-and-Deacons-in-the-United-States-1950-2002.pdf.

9. Sexual Abuse Task Force, "Guidepost Solutions' Report of the Independent Investigation," Guidepost Solutions, May 22, 2022, https://www.sataskforce.net/updates/guidepost-solutions-report-of-the-independent-investigation.

behavior are completely disqualified from ministry. There is no place for abuse of any kind in the church. The church is designed by God to be the safest of places. Jesus sees these abusers for who they are, and they will stand accountable in this life and the next for their actions.

As Christians, we should be the loudest voices affirming the concern of those who distrust the church because of illegitimate leaders who perpetrate and perpetuate any kind of abuse in the church. So, how do we counsel them? After listening to, affirming, and weeping with them, we can walk slowly with them toward what Jesus really intends for his people.

Certainly, these people need to be connected with qualified professionals to help them work through their trauma. It is okay for someone who has experienced abuse in the church to be slow to go back. They need Christian community, but it can start with a small group outside of the corporate gathering like a prayer group or a Bible study. When the time is right, this person should not go to church alone, but with trusted friends.

And it's okay for them to be leery upon return. They should be! They should ask the right questions. What does accountability look like for the leaders in the church? How has this church addressed issues like these in the past? What kind of policies are in place when taking care of children? How does the leadership respond to their story? They should ask these hard questions all the while leaning into Jesus for strength and wisdom in this precarious journey.

The challenging journey back will be worth it. In the words of Ann Voskamp, "Shame dies when stories are told in safe places."[10] May we be safe places inside and outside the church for those who have been wounded. While there is no silver bullet to prevent abuse 100 percent of the time, there are many churches in this country that

10. Ann Voskamp, "Shame dies when stories are told in safe places," Twitter, October 3, 2016, 9:52 a.m., https://twitter.com/annvoskamp/status/782941512061575168?lang=en.

value accountability and transparency and create a culture where the least among us are truly safe. People who dechurched because of abuse need to hear that the protection, integrity, and justice they desire is what Jesus desires as well, and that there is a church nearby where they can not only be safe but be a real part of bringing safety to those who need it the most. What a blessing it is for people to bring their hurt and their story to make others safer.

The Isolation Issue: You Need the Church (and the Church Needs You)

I (Jim) have a friend who is a Christian but has stopped going to church because "even before the pandemic, we were just so crazy busy with our kids' activities that Sunday was the only morning when we could actually rest. There are a lot of easy and convenient excuses to selfishly avoid a massive storm on Sunday mornings." This friend, sadly, is in good company as 11 percent of those in our study said that attending church just became inconvenient. Again, when we focused on dechurched evangelicals, that number rose to 17 percent. Fourteen percent said they had other priorities for their time and money, which brings to mind a woman at a local coffee shop I frequent. She is a Christian and said she "moved to Orlando and hit the ground running and just never plugged into a church." She now has other priorities on Sunday morning and may return one day but has no plans to do so anytime soon.

As a father of four, I (Jim) can certainly appreciate the busyness of our culture. I can appreciate how hard it is to move and find a new church family. I can even appreciate how unique COVID-19 was as it freed up Sundays to play golf, go to the beach, or just sleep in. Even so, these dechurched Christians need to hear that they need the church.

The author of Hebrews wrote, "Let us consider how to stir up one another to love and good works, not neglecting to meet together, as is the habit of some, but encouraging one another, and all the more as you see the Day drawing near" (Heb. 10:24–25). Being substantively plugged into a local church with committed relationships in a defined group of people is God's plan for Christians to carry out the "one anothers" and grow in Christlikeness. It helps us guard against arrogance, isolation, and flakiness.

At my (Jim's) former church, I knew a woman who, outside of the church, I probably never would have interacted with. She became a Christian and brought with her a very hard life full of physical, emotional, and material needs. Families in the church would have her over to do her laundry, make her meals, talk through her challenging circumstances, and pray. They would even provide money for her rent and utilities. After a couple of years of this, she took her life. I'll never forget attending her funeral and hearing the pastor, J. D. Shaw, say, "Amanda taught us how to love." In that moment, it hit me like a ton of bricks that whatever blessing Amanda received from the church, we received more.

We need the church. I need the church. The church draws us more deeply toward real relationships, deeper love, and true humanity. In the words of Collin Hansen and Jonathan Leeman, "No one gets the church they want, but everyone gets the church they need."[11]

Not only do you miss out if you are not in physical relational contact with the church, but the church misses out by not having you. It's hard to fully appreciate the communal nature of the church when we read the Bible in English. If we were to read the DSV (Deep South Version) of the Bible, we would clearly see that "y'all are the temple. Y'all are the city on a hill. Y'all are the body of Christ." We are the church, and we are not fully "we" without you.

---

11. Jonathan Leeman and Collin Hansen, *Rediscover Church: Why the Body of Christ Is Essential* (Wheaton, IL: Crossway, 2021), 143.

The Belief Issue:
The Gospel Is Good News

The largest reason people gave for leaving the church (23%) was a change in belief of some kind. They may have left a church for good reasons. They may have heard true, negative things about the church. Their sexual ethic may have changed, creating a crisis of faith. They may have experienced tragic things at the hands of the leaders in a church that caused them to doubt the message those leaders taught. But also hear this: the gospel is good news.

We all are enslaved by our own sin. We are born into this world rebellious. We are guilty before God of claiming to know how to better run our lives. We are guilty of declaring ourselves to be a better god. Sin is not the bad decisions we make. Sin is the disease inside of us that causes us to make bad, self-destructive decisions. That is the bad news, and it is why Jesus came.

Jesus, the second person of the Trinity, humbled himself by taking on flesh to live the perfect life we cannot. He experienced every temptation we do yet remained sinless. He went to the cross to receive the full wrath of God we deserve in our place and then gave us his righteousness. Everything the perfect Son of God merited with his perfect life, he freely gives to us. Three days later, he resurrected, powerfully declaring to the world that he has defeated death for those who place their trust in him. Death for the believer is not a doorway into the wrath we deserve, but into an eternity of grace, mercy, and love with our Creator.

When we place our trust in Jesus, we become a part of his body—not simply metaphorically, but in some real, mysterious way. We are bound to each other the way a hand is bound to an arm or an eye to a face. We call this body the church. The church, for now, is still imperfect. We will experience disappointment and, at times, disgrace, but it is still God's design for his people. Jesus tells us there will be weeds among the wheat and wolves in sheep's clothing, and he will deal with that at the appropriate time. But whatever disappointment or harm you have experienced in the church, a greater blessing awaits you there.

If the gospel is good news to you, the church is your body and your family. There is no greater message the dechurched need to hear than this. The gospel is good news, and it brings us together.

Part 4

Lessons for
the Church

Chapter 12

Spiritual Formation and the Dechurched

WE ARE IN A CRISIS OF SPIRITUAL FORMATION.

We are in a crisis of spiritual formation *because* we live in an attention economy.

Attention *is* money.

Through a 2020 *Wall Street Journal* article concerning leaked internal Facebook corporate memos, we learned, "Our algorithms exploit the human brain's attraction to divisiveness. . . . If left unchecked," Facebook would feed users "more and more divisive content in an effort to gain more user attention & increase time on the platform."[1]

Facebook needs you to stay on their platform longer so it can serve you more ads, so it can earn more profit, so it can generate more value for shareholders. Attention. Money. Profit. Shareholders. Repeat. If the most efficient way to make you pay attention is to serve up stuff that will make you mad and stay on longer, they will, because the shareholders (which ironically might also be you deep in

---

1. Jeff Horwitz, "Facebook Executives Shut Down Efforts to Make the Site Less Divisive," *Wall Street Journal*, May 26, 2020, https://www.wsj.com/articles/facebook-knows-it-encourages-division-top-executives-nixed-solutions-11590507499.

some mutual fund or exchange-traded fund) demand it. Large companies will give away their services to you because *you are the product*, and they need to serve you as many ads as possible. They will be largely agnostic on what those ads are as long as they don't create a public relations mess.

Every proprietary algorithm at all of the large tech and social media companies has discovered what the Bible has already told us about the human condition. We are inherently prone to division, strife, and anger. We will sit for long periods of time and consume content that puts our brains into a cortisol state and makes it increasingly difficult to be renewed in our minds and to embody the fruit of the Spirit.

Our pastor friend Patrick Miller put a fine point on this truth pastorally:

> Like every other pastor in America, I'm wrestling with a new challenge. Artificial intelligence—using neural networks and sophisticated machine-learning algorithms—is shepherding my church into the valley of the shadow of death. The algorithm, to misquote Psalm 139, has searched them and known their hearts. It tests them and measures their anxious thoughts. It has woven digital models of them in its silicon womb so it can sell their everlasting data to the highest bidder and keep them addicted to the online platform it serves.[2]

Information Diet

Consider for a moment that every person you meet doesn't just have a food diet but also has an information diet. People will consume

---

2. Patrick Miller, "'I Lost My Mom to Facebook,'" TGC, August 24, 2022, https://www.thegospelcoalition.org/article/lost-mom-facebook-shepherd-algorithms/.

social media, podcasts, YouTube, radio, books, blogs, television, and movies. Whether we realize it or not, this volume of information is constantly forming and shaping our vision of what is true, good, and beautiful. Compound the information diet with algorithm-fed division for profit.

How much of your information diet is consumed with any meta-awareness of *why* the content is being shown to you?

How much of your information diet is consumed with any meta-awareness of *what* that content is *doing* to your soul?

How much of your information diet is consumed with any meta-awareness of *how much credibility* you give that content?

Having increased ability to zoom out on these questions will give us increased cognizance and comprehensive vision in terms of how much influence we should ascribe to the various voices in our information diet. Let's continue down that path with an additional tool on how to make the subconscious more cognizant.

Influence Multiplier

Every one of us constantly makes assessments of the content and people with whom we interact. The way in which we assign an amount of influence to the ideas or person is largely subconscious. That subconscious assessment will magnify, diminish, or negate the influence of the content or person. For example, let's say you take a particular thought leader very seriously. You might subconsciously afford that person several times more influence than an average person. Another person or set of ideas you might not take very seriously, and you afford that person or set of ideas little to no influence. Finally, there are people whom you distrust, and when they try to influence you, their actions have the opposite of their intended effect. Altogether there are probably five categories of subconscious influence multipliers:

1. Very influential
2. Influential
3. Average influence
4. Below average influence
5. Negative influence

Susan

Let's take, for example, Susan, who is churched and who *really* likes her pastor. She sees her pastor as being in the very influential category and makes sure she never misses his thirty-minute weekly sermon. Let's say Susan also attends a small group for ninety minutes a week, and it is in the influential category for her.

Outside of church, Susan's weekly information diet includes fourteen hours of cable news, fourteen hours of social media scrolling, seven hours of web surfing, ten hours of streaming content, two hours of podcasts, an hour of YouTube, three hours of radio, and two hours of books.

When you compare Susan's two church-centric time blocks with the sheer volume of other things forming and shaping her throughout the week, the time in church pales in comparison. Even if she considers her pastor's sermons and her small group at the highest level of influence, her church time is still completely overshadowed by the rest of her information diet.

The crisis of spiritual formation is unavoidable. No one is influential enough to overcome the sheer volume of other things influencing even the most faithful people in their church. We have seen how this dynamic has been particularly challenging for those who are clergy. Anecdotally, many clergy we've spoken with feel that their task has become impossible, even Sisyphean[3] at points. Hence, Susan's spiritual health will rise and fall based on the extent to which

---

3. A Sisyphean task is something that is impossible to complete. The phrase comes from the character Sisyphus in Homer's *Iliad*, who has been consigned by the gods to perpetually roll a rock up a hill, then let it roll down that hill, only to repeat the cycle.

her outside-the-church information diet is consonant or dissonant with God's vision for truth, goodness, and beauty.

Max

Now let's take, for example, Max, who is dechurched and is actively questioning evangelical subculture. These things have Max in a disoriented state as he is trying to sort out everything. Max has a similar information diet as Susan in regard to media, but his diet primarily consists of voices that highlight evangelical hypocrisy, unholy political alliances, and ethical inconsistencies. He has had some bad experiences in church that have reinforced the critiques he is hearing. He no longer belongs to a church, yet he still believes the core tenets of the faith and behaves with his prior ethical norms.

Susan and Max are not merely receiving content. Thought patterns are being normalized. Desires are reshaping. Hurts are being answered. Hopes are being validated. At their very cores, they are being formed. This formative process is happening beneath the surface in our friends inside and outside the church who have bought into unhelpful narratives from the secular left, the secular right, and maybe even conspiracy theories with no basis in reality.

We ought to have increased awareness of *why* digital content is being shown to us. We need to realize that some of these algorithms are so fine-tuned that media companies already know what things we are more likely to stop and look at longer, or are more inclined to click, or are more likely to get worked up over so that we stay inside their ecosystem longer and can be fed more ads to serve their bottom line and shareholders.

We should also be cognizant of and vigilant concerning what consumption of our information diet is doing to us. Whether it is cable news running for hours on end in the background, the latest foolishness that has been shared by a group or person with whom you strongly disagree, or anything you watch just to numb yourself after a long or stressful day—all these things are doing something to you and your soul. More often than not these things are misshaping you into something unhealthy.

We should also be awake to how much credibility we are attributing to various sources. Ascribing more weight and value to digital or TV personalities than we do to the human beings whom we've been in relationship and community with for years is dangerous. Yes, everyone in real life has their quirks, but at least we can account for those things accordingly in terms of how much credibility and influence we ascribe.

Part of our task in this cultural moment is to help people pursue healthier information diets. When I was growing up, my mom always said, "Garbage in, garbage out." There is a whole mess of garbage in our culture that would contort us and misshape us into all sorts of foolishness. It takes a lot of wisdom to see errors coming at you from all directions and to put off those errors and continue to walk the path of wisdom. Hence, a key part of both our own discipleship and caring for dechurched people is pursuing information diets that are increasingly healthy and wise, and that promote human flourishing.

The Two-Chapter Gospel versus the Four-Chapter Gospel

As we think about pursuing greater health in our information diets, what better place to start than making sure that our understanding of the gospel of Jesus Christ is correct? Broadly speaking, the Christian faith consists of a four-chapter gospel:[4]

1. **CREATION:** God made everything, and it was good.
2. **FALL:** Man sinned, and everything became cursed.

---

4. Timothy Keller, "Tim Keller Explains the Gospel," Acts 29, December 12, 2008, https://www.acts29.com/tim-keller-explains-the-gospel/.

3. **REDEMPTION:** Jesus saves sinners and inaugurates his kingdom.
4. **CONSUMMATION:** Jesus consummates his kingdom, and all of creation is recreated.

When we zoom out, we see that different segments of the world in different large seasons have emphasized certain chapters of this four-chapter gospel more than others. Twentieth-century evangelicalism primarily focused on a two-chapter gospel of fall and redemption.[5] The message was one of personal salvation through Jesus for individuals so they could be spared from hell and be resurrected with Christ. While this message is true, it is a truncated gospel. When we lose emphasis on chapters 1 and 4, we lose the cosmic vision for the extent of what God is doing in creation. God is making all things new (Rev. 21:1–8), and redemption will come as far as the curse is found. A two-chapter gospel will have a hard time connecting the dots regarding the importance of addressing the overall health of the movement, particularly as it pertains to legitimate criticism levied against it.

In Luke 15 Jesus gave the parable of the prodigal son. In that parable, we see two brothers who are lost: a younger brother who is prone to loose morals and an older brother who is a strict rule follower. A two-chapter gospel somewhat worked when America was more of a "younger-brother" culture with tremendous moral laxity. The problems of guilt and shame can be remedied by the cross of Christ and the resurrection. True enough.

However, a two-chapter gospel is insufficient for the increasingly "older-brother" culture of the early twenty-first century. You may have noticed that in the West, broadly speaking we have shifted from a more younger-brother, libertine and licentious culture of the 1960s–2001—the sexual revolution, free-market everything—to

---

5. Keller.

a more older-brother, justice-minded culture in the post–9/11 world—#MeToo, Black Lives Matter, and a host of other lenses that reexamine the interplay of power and ethics. There has been a hard turn culturally in the West toward justice and ethics. The internet, social media, and other democratizing forces have leveled the power pyramid and made people aware of the animating concerns of the marginalized, disenfranchised, and disinherited. The two-chapter gospel is an anemic message for an older-brother culture because it fails to tell the whole story. As mentioned earlier, this culture's questions are more about whether Jesus is good and beautiful and less about whether he is true. Only a four-chapter gospel will suffice in an older-brother culture. The pain point is less the soul-felt burden of individual sin and more a burden of what vision promotes human flourishing and discourages injustice. Another way to think about the differences of a two- versus four-chapter gospel is the difference between a "tell me" versus a "show me" approach to gospel procla- mation. There were times in the twentieth century when all you had to do was invite your friends to an event like a Billy Graham crusade and many would respond to the gospel. This is a classic two-chapter "tell me" approach. These days are almost entirely gone in America, and in both the data and our pastoral experiences, we've seen that before most folks believe, they need to experience the gospel tangibly through some combination of connecting to Christian community and seeing Christians exercise their beliefs in ways that show that Christianity actively promotes human flourishing.

A Way Forward

The good news is that the church has long possessed a four-chapter gospel, and we have experienced times when the church has proven to be quite strong and healthy. Rodney Stark's landmark work, *The Rise of Christianity*, demonstrates that the "central doctrines of

Christianity prompted sustained attractive, liberating, and effective social relations and organizations."[6] The early church existed in the margins of society and endured tremendous waves of persecution. Christians were some of the only people to stay in cities devastated by deadly plagues. The early church treated women with a dignity that was radically countercultural for that time. The church leaned into the challenges of their ethnic, socioeconomic, and cultural differences to create a curious community.

At the corporate level, Christianity in the West will have to recapture many facets of this kind of Christianity that exist at the bottom of the power pyramid. Secularism will continue to wash over the West in both its left and right manifestations, and Christians who wish to remain faithful will seek alliances with neither. These things will leave us ministering from a place of increasing vulnerability and declining power. However, as we can see from our brothers and sisters in East Asia, an increased cost of discipleship sometimes accelerates the fruitfulness and plausibility of the gospel.

Imago Dei is a theological term that refers to the fact that humanity is made in the image of God. That image endows great dignity, meaning, worth, and value on every human being regardless of anything outward about that person or in relation to their utility to culture, society, or marketplace. Bearing God's image denotes intrinsic value. Hence, on the corporate level, we need to grow in our understanding of the *imago Dei*, address legitimate ethical concerns, and embrace our diminished power in society.[7] As cultural power continues to shift, ministry leaders in particular must grow in their ability to disciple people through the loss of that power.

On the individual level, we return to what Paul wrote in his

6. Rodney Stark, *The Rise of Christianity: How the Obscure, Marginal Jesus Movement Became the Dominant Religious Force in the Western World in a Few Centuries* (Princeton, NJ: Princeton University Press, 1996; repr., San Francisco: HarperSanFrancisco, 2020), 211.

7. Timothy Keller, *How to Reach the West Again* (New York: Redeemer City to City, 2020), 21–32.

letter to Timothy: "You therefore, my son, be strong in the grace that is in Christ Jesus. The things which you have heard from me in the presence of many witnesses, entrust these to faithful people who will be able to teach others also" (2 Tim. 2:1–2 NASB).

Content, Context, and Habit

Reshaping people's information diet with healthier content won't be enough. We are not merely brains. Consider what James K. A. Smith ponders in the preface of his book *You Are What You Love*:

> What if, instead of starting with the assumption that human beings are thinking things, we started from the conviction that human beings are first and foremost *lovers*? What if you are defined not by what you know but by what you *desire*? What if the center and seat of the human person is found not in the heady regions of the intellect but in the gut-level regions of the heart? How would that change our approach to discipleship and Christian formation?[8]

We need content, context, and habit. If you are living off a steady diet of deconstructing streams of the secular left or fundamentalist streams of Christian nationalism, then getting off a junk-food information diet is critical.

But how do we do this?

We need the context of safe, transparent, and vulnerable relationships with emotionally, culturally, and spiritually mature brothers and sisters in the faith. Those relationships need to be intimate enough to cut through the mess of all the influence multipliers of any of the unhealthy aspects of our information diet. Those relationships need to be gracious and patient enough to give time and space for the

---

8. James K. A. Smith, *You Are What You Love* (Grand Rapids: Brazos, 2016), 7.

formation we seek. Those relationships need to be deep enough to get into the habits and routines of our lives so that we remake our habits in ways that promote spiritual vitality, kingdom ethics, and human flourishing.

Our information diet is not all that different from our cardiovascular system. The human body contains three kinds of blood vessels: arteries, veins, and capillaries. Arteries take oxygen-rich blood to various broad parts of the body. Capillaries take the oxygen-rich blood into the deepest recesses of the body where oxygen and carbon dioxide are swapped. The capillaries then connect to veins, which carry the carbon-dioxide rich blood back to the heart. We need all three kinds of blood vessels in order to live.

Consider for a moment that the preached Word is like arteries carrying oxygen-rich blood to broad areas of our person. Discipleship and spiritual formation are like the capillaries in that they take gospel-infused wisdom into the deepest recesses of the body where truth replaces lies, goodness replaces harm, and beauty replaces ugliness. Veins are the only blood vessels with one-way valves. As such, veins function like a gentle and loving church community that always encourages us to take our idols back to God, who meets us yet again with more of his true, good, and beautiful gospel. Our veins' one-way valves help provide some gentle correction to keep the blood flowing in the right direction back to the oxygenating source so that the whole body might continue being cyclically enriched with life-giving nutrients.

Blood vessels function in a system. When that system is working properly, it provides health and vitality for the whole person. But when there is disease in the system, the body will suffer, sometimes catastrophically.

An uncomfortable amount of the evangelical world suffers from a kind of cardiovascular disease. Earthly political alliances became indiscernible from our efforts for the kingdom of God. In some instances, those unholy alliances created hidden necrosis in the body, which spread into systemic body-wide catastrophe. Unduly narrow visions of "pro-life" created a lot of valid criticism of how we treat those outside the womb. Unchecked patriarchy created great harm and trauma for many. A failure to name, properly adjudicate, and pro-actively prevent sexual abuse caused irreparable damage. A failure to see dignity in LGBTQ+ persons altered a national conversation that could have been approached differently. Those who sought to address racism at the personal and structural levels were labeled, maligned, and sometimes slandered. Pastoral misconduct gave many plenty of reasons to paint evangelicals as hypocrites. Institutions failed to deal equitably with people in a variety of circumstances. If we wish for people to return to church, we need to make sure that we are building churches and institutions that are healthy. A healthy local church will be one that strives to be increasingly growing in our true, good, and beautiful gospel.

Cardiovascular Sickness and the Dechurched

Cardiovascular sickness is not hard to see if you are willing to look at doctors' charts. We need a fully orbed gospel that emphasizes God's true, good, and beautiful vision for humanity. If evangelicalism doesn't begin to take greater ownership and address the problems within its own movement, the consequences will continue to be serious. We cannot control people's disordered wants and idols, but we can stop the rate at which we are scoring goals on ourselves.

There must be a vigorous pursuit of the authentic Jesus of the Bible. All counterfeit versions of Jesus must be removed: prosperity Jesus, white American Jesus, shock jock Jesus, and a dozen other caricatures. We must return to the teachings of Jesus in the kingdom parables, the Sermon on the Mount, and Jesus' interactions with religious leaders to see what kind of person he is and what kind of kingdom he is creating. The individualistic two-chapter gospel will be insufficient in the older-brother West. Only the full four-chapter gospel will suffice for an increasingly skeptical world that is more concerned with whether our Jesus is good and beautiful and true.

When talking with friends or neighbors who have a strong pull to a secular left utopian vision, we don't need to freak out in our souls and bemoan the death of America. While the desire for justice, equity, and human flourishing are good, those desires and impulses can't be found through the secular left avenues employed. In judo, instead of going toe-to-toe trading punches, you redirect the momentum and inertia of your opponent. These are judo conversations, not boxing matches.

When you know people who are deconstructing, dechurching, or even deconverting, don't pull away from those relationships. Lean into them by asking open, curious questions, and then listen. There are probably many areas where we can find common ground and agree on problems within our movement. When you hear such things, you can say, "I agree with you; these are problems." Sometimes people just need someone else to validate dysfunctional things and tell them they aren't crazy. Obviously, we can't ever affirm people in their sin and idolatry, but we can be people who love others where they are and not abandon the relationship. This is precisely where we employ the comprehend, commend, and critique framework we introduced in chapter 11, "Messages for the Dechurched."

We lean into these relationships. We listen. We validate where we can validate. We challenge people not to throw out the baby with the bathwater. We bring them back to the authentic Jesus. If we are going to lose people (and we will), let's make sure we are only losing them to the Jesus of the Bible.

In our fictitious story earlier in the chapter, Susan may need to take a ninety-day fast from cable news and political talk radio. She probably needs to avoid doom scrolling.[9] She definitely needs to read her Bible, pray, serve others, and be in community with others doing the same thing with the time she has redeemed from her fasting.

Max needs an embodied community to work through the angst in his soul. He needs some folks who don't have a culturally captive faith who will show a better way between various counterfeit versions of Jesus. We want Max to see that he can disenculturate his faith by patiently separating problematic subculture from the gospel of Jesus Christ.

Both Susan and Max need a full four-chapter gospel, a healthy information diet, deep relationships that sharpen, and daily renewal from Jesus. We must preach a four-chapter gospel to ourselves before guiding Susan or Jonathan to the missing chapters. When we lean into that four-chapter gospel, we can begin to address our present crisis of spiritual formation. Only when the influence of Scripture, Jesus, and the Holy Spirit outweigh in both time and multiplier can we begin a journey of finding wholeness and being conformed into the image of Christ (Rom. 8:29).

---

9. The act of willfully spending time focusing on negative news.

Chapter 13

Confessional and Missional

IN 2023 THE NFL SALARY CAP FOR EACH TEAM WAS $224.8 MILLION.
That means a team cannot spend more than that amount on all of its
players' salaries combined.[1] Imagine for a moment that an NFL team
decided to spend $210 million on their offense and only $14.8 million
on their defense. Or imagine if another team did the exact opposite,
choosing to prioritize its defense. The fans would be outraged, and
the team would certainly not be successful. Well, this is essentially
what many churches do.

A Tale of Two Churches

Imagine two churches in the same American city: Redeemer
Confessional Church and Grace Missional Church. Redeemer
Confessional Church is a bedrock of theological teaching. It has a

---

1. Mark Lane, "NFL 2023 Salary Cap: Which Teams Have the Most, Least Space?," Yahoo!
Sports, February 24, 2023, https://sports.yahoo.com/nfl-2023-salary-cap-teams-110038797.html.

high view of church membership, congregational worship, discipleship, and both teaching and preaching. The problem, though, is that while this church is theologically faithful, it is missionally challenged. Twelve percent of the dechurched evangelicals we surveyed said that a factor in their decision to leave was that they didn't see the congregation doing enough good in the community. The church felt insular.

Redeemer Confessional Church is dedicated to its overseas partners and faithfully supports missionaries in other parts of the world but struggles to see missional fruit in its own city. This church baptizes few believers that aren't biologically related to someone in the church. In fact, when their missionaries come back to visit, they note that the worship service feels inaccessible, the sermons are hard to understand or boring, and the music feels outdated. They are faithful to teaching the right theology but missing the hearts of the people in the pews. Redeemer Confessional Church has a love of content over context. They are a church that embraces confession at the expense of mission.

Down the street is Grace Missional Church, a very popular church in town. It features music that young people enjoy and messages that are moving and engaging. Many people who attend Grace would never enter Redeemer Confessional Church, and most of them don't even know it exists. Grace baptizes large numbers of people and serves the local schools in many ways. But they struggle to go very deep theologically, and they avoid topics that might cause discomfort for people who attend. Even though they seem to baptize many more people, those baptized represent less than a third of those who make professions of faith, showing that true discipleship is lacking. The lion's share of the efforts of the church leaders and the money donated goes to creating a worship experience that people will want to be a part of. Grace Missional Church has a love of context over content. They embrace mission over confession.

The Danger of
Confession-Only Church

While no church perfectly engages both confession and mission, many churches embrace one at the expense of the other. In the church in Ephesus, Scripture gives us a clear warning for the church that embraces confession at the expense of mission.

We know as much or more about the Ephesian church than we do any other church of its time. Luke told us about its beginning in Acts, Paul wrote a whole letter to them, and John recorded Jesus' address to them in Revelation. Ephesus had one heck of a start. Basically, it was every church planter's dream. People were converted, the miracles and healings were so great that the itinerant Jewish exorcists (an interesting group to be sure) decided to try and do their thing in Jesus' name (which did not go well), and people were so repentant that it changed the whole economy of Ephesus. Riots began to break out because people were burning their expensive books of dark arts and refusing to give money to idols. Luke recorded that at one point every person in the city had heard the name of Jesus.

Ephesus was a fortress of good doctrine. We have letters from the early church fathers talking about how Ephesus was not a place where heresy could thrive. But by the time we get to Revelation 2, it seems their zeal for doctrine had become greater than their love for Jesus (Rev. 2:2–4). Jesus told them they had lost the love they had at first.

When a church gets more excited about being right than reaching hearts, it has become confessional at the expense of the mission. When a church has more zeal for right doctrine than for showing people Jesus, it has lost its first love. Walls go up. It no longer sees itself as sent into the world but focuses only on protecting itself and its doctrine from a hostile world that could grab us and our children at any moment. If love for Jesus and the people he came to redeem is toppled by a love for right doctrine, that will create an insular, prideful church. A church that loses its first love, Jesus, then loses love for its neighbor, which is replaced by a prideful love of being right.

Prideful churches begin to elevate secondary and tertiary issues to a primary conviction. They are threatened by people who don't see the world the same way. They are threatened by other Christians who don't look and act like them. And prideful churches die. This is exactly what Jesus threatened the Ephesian church with when he said, "Remember therefore from where you have fallen; repent, and do the works you did at first. If not, I will come to you and remove your lampstand from its place, unless you repent" (Rev. 2:5). Any church that has a specific doctrinal or cultural flag flying higher than the flag of Jesus will not survive.

Questions for the Confession-Only Church

Here are a few practical questions to see if you might be trending confessional at the expense of missional. What shapes your worldview more, the people you engage or the pages you read? If your worldview is more informed by words from outside the Bible (whether books or social media) more than real people, your heart will grow cold. It's easy to sit behind a computer screen and read articles about the people you disagree with. It's much harder to get to know people who are different from you and do the heavy lifting of understanding them in hopes of prayerfully showing them Jesus.

Ask yourself, does your content intersect your context? I (Jim) have a friend who I consider to be a Christian leader in his city. The pastor of a declining church in a growing area of town came to him lamenting the lack of traction his church had with younger people. My friend's response was loving but direct. He said, "It's because your church isn't giving them helpful biblical answers to the questions they are asking. Your church doesn't understand the culture they live in enough to give them helpful answers from the Bible." We need to become students of this world. We need to exegete our context as well as we exegete our Bibles. A church that is both confessional and missional is going to break down the walls that the world has built to keep us out.

In our desire to enter and engage this world, are we listening more than we are speaking? Missional living in the twentieth century had more to do with a transfer of information. This led to evangelistic strategies like the Four Laws and the Roman Road and a whole system of apologetics that attempted to reason people into the faith. Those resources have blessed us in many ways, but we now live in a context where it is often unhelpful to use those resources as our first foot forward. If we approach someone with more talking than listening, we are more confessional than missional. In fact, the skill set of a qualified counselor may do more to fuel evangelism than our classic apologetic methods.

We need to listen well and ask curious, caring questions to know people well enough to introduce them to Jesus. Thirty percent of the dechurched evangelicals we polled said they wished their parents had simply listened more. The church as a whole would do well to heed that advice. The most meaningful and helpful introductions happen when you know the two people you're introducing. The same is true in evangelism. If we don't know both parties, while we can still make an introduction, it is just going to be more awkward and less fruitful.

The Danger of Mission-Only Church

On the other hand, the love of context over content leads the way to inappropriate cultural accommodation—a watering down of what we believe in hopes of gaining traction with lost people. The evangelistic heart of missional-only churches is commendable but misguided, and Scripture tells this story as well. Maybe the earliest example we have of this kind of church is in Pergamum, also in Revelation 2.

Pergamum was a city in the heart of pagan worship. It was also the capital of the Roman province of Asia. It had to be one of the hardest places for a church to exist. The very existence of a church there would have been a testament to the power of Jesus. But there was a problem. The church had begun to allow its people to practice sexual immorality and embrace the false teachings of the Nicolaitans. In other words, the church was accommodating the practices of the culture.

We must ask the question, why is it that the church in Pergamum was allowing these kinds of cultural accommodations? Likely, it was the only way they would grow numerically. They lived in a culture where it was extremely difficult to walk with Christ. This is precisely why Jesus said, "I know where you dwell" (Rev. 2:13). It's as if Jesus was saying, "I know how hard it is to reach people in your city. I get it. But you can't stray from my clear teachings to reach them." This was a church that had gone to an extreme of mission at the expense of confession. There was more love for the context than the confession. They traded the clear teachings of God for cultural accommodation.

Questions for the Mission-Only Church

This issue at hand is cultural accommodation, and we would like to probe it in three areas: in belief, in style, and in proximity to the local church. Is your church minimizing or even letting go of important doctrines to accommodate the changing culture? All of the seven historic mainline Protestant denominations in the United

States—the Presbyterian Church (USA), American Baptists, the United Methodist Church, the Episcopal Church, the United Church of Christ, Disciples of Christ, and the Evangelical Lutheran Church in America—have had to battle cultural accommodation in belief as science and technology advanced. The pressure began in Germany in the 1700s but made its way into our seminaries in the early twentieth century. At first the miracles of the Bible were in question: if things like the sun standing still, the Red Sea parting, the virgin birth, and the resurrection of Jesus can't happen under natural law, they must be false.

Then the exclusivity of Jesus came into question. This gave rise to views of all religions basically being the same thing, with Jesus being just one of the ways to God. Which is, of course, the exact opposite of what Jesus taught. He said, "I am the way, and the truth, and the life. No one comes to the Father except through me" (John 14:6). Increasingly throughout the twentieth and twenty-first centuries, in the mainline churches other views are tolerated at the expense of Jesus being the only way.

Later sexual ethics began to change. This is how J. D. Shaw put it:

[This is] how it probably happened in Pergamum: a group in the church said, "Of course, we must obey God. We must follow him and be faithful to the Scriptures. But the Scriptures were written in Israel, by Jews, and for Jews, and we need to take that into account. We are Greek and Roman gentiles—we are believers in Jesus, but we are different from those folks in Israel. We think what the Bible says about sex is culturally bound. Those teachings were never meant to apply to all people at all times. And if the Jewish writers of the Scriptures knew what life was like in Pergamum, well they would have never said that sex was only to be had between a man and a woman inside of marriage. There are too many temptations in Pergamum, too many temple prostitutes, too many available women. So we need to reinterpret the Scriptures in light of our time and place, and give ourselves a break. After all, we know in our hearts we belong to Jesus."[2]

Second, is your church theologically orthodox, but out of a desire to attract and/or retain people, do you deprioritize teaching things that could be seen as offensive? This is an issue of style, because it's not about what you believe; it's about how you don't teach it. I (Jim) have a pastor friend who once told me that a large number of unmarried but cohabiting couples attended his church, and that when it came to teaching a biblical sexual ethic, he could never teach that cohabitation was wrong because he was afraid they would not come back. To his credit, many of these people would not have walked into most of the churches in our city, so there is much to admire, but there must be a plan to disciple them even if (and especially if) that is not happening in Sunday worship.

We commend the desire for the gospel to go forward, but if we are unwilling to teach the full counsel of God, we create a low spiritual ceiling, which limits the joy, satisfaction, and fruitfulness we experience in the Christian life. We commend the desire in churches to have a large front door back into the church, but the data shows that if we hold back in our discipleship, we could instead become a last stop through the back door as people aren't given what they need to follow Christ in an increasingly difficult culture. We would never buy our children laser tag equipment and then send them into a real battle, but we do a similar thing when we deprioritize equipping the saints and send them into the world. We would do well to hear Jesus' encouraging words to the church in Pergamum: "I know where you dwell." This isn't a threat that he will show up and do harm while you are in bed; it is a gentle acknowledgment that he understands how hard it is to live in this world and that he will be with us every step of the way.

---

2. J. D. Shaw, "Pergamum: Living in the World," Grace Bible Church, May 21, 2017, https://gracebibleofoxford.com/messages/that-you-may-believe/.

Third, is the ministry you are engaged in substantively connected to the local church? My (Jim's) first four years of ministry were in Europe with a global evangelistic ministry. I'm very thankful for those years. God introduced to me some of the most influential people in my life who have become dear friends. I grew in my personal evangelism, knowledge of the Bible, and personal holiness. God grew me in my faith in incredible ways during those years, but there was one significant flaw. Dozens of American missionaries devoted their lives to that ministry. Hundreds of students were exposed to the gospel and involved in our ministry. But today I am not aware of a single person native to that country who is any closer to Jesus because of our work there.

So, what was that flaw? We were missional, but we weren't connected to any local church. At the time, there wasn't a single church in the whole city we could attend. We were a "parachurch" ministry that wasn't actually coming alongside any church. We needed a church with native believers to whom we could connect the people we were reaching and from whom we could learn. Years later we went back and did the same work in the same country, but alongside an Acts 29 church plant, and ten years later, this church is thriving and 100 percent led by natives of that country.

This is just one story, but we've seen similar patterns in high school, college, and professional ministries around the country that do not prioritize connecting the people in these ministries to the local church. We have talked with pastors who observe young professionals who were involved in a campus ministry in college struggle to connect to a local church after graduation because it is so different from what they experienced doing life with a hundred other students in their same stage of life. As we mentioned in chapter 10, the students in our survey who were involved both in a campus ministry and a local church were three times more likely to stay connected to a local church later in life. If our work is not connected to the church, why would we expect the fruit of it to be?

Adding Mission to Confession

When we say "missional," we aren't primarily talking about global missions, although that is certainly included. The term *missional* means much more. It speaks to how we engage our fallen world. To put all our cards on the table, for the past four years, this is what we have worked to do at Orlando Grace Church. The pastor before me (Jim) is one of the most faithful pastors I have ever known. He invested deeply in the confessional side of our church, and as he was retiring, he urged the church leadership to find someone to follow him who would build missional onto the confessional foundation. As that pastor, I could not have been more blessed by his vision and humility.

In our own context, we have had to ask hard questions about why we have so many theologically developed people but so few conversions and baptisms. We had to reassess every area of our discipleship programs. We developed classes about how our confession is actually a missional document. We assessed the accessibility of our worship. We aren't becoming less confessional; we are adding mission to the confession. One of the most important things we are trying to do is equip our people to go out into the world and live missional lives.

You've likely heard the phrase "in the world but not of the world." This idea comes from John 17 and has been manipulated to say two things Jesus was not saying. Some have used it to say that we need to adopt more of the world inside the church. We've seen people take up cigarette smoking to try to embody this idea more. This is an example of overstating Jesus' intentions of what it means to be in the world. The other extreme is to say, "Unfortunately, we live in this fallen world, but we need to build barriers between us and the world. We need to build barriers between this world and our children. Between this world and our doctrine." At its worst, this creates an insular environment where we don't know how to properly engage this world because we just aren't in it. We could become like

Rhino the hamster in the movie *Bolt*, who moves about the world but never leaves the inside of his hamster ball. This attitude toward the world fails to prepare our children to enter it well, and it fails to reach those outside the church.

Jesus said in John 17:14–18, "I have given them your word, and the world has hated them because they are not of the world, just as I am not of the world. I do not ask that you take them out of the world, but that you keep them from the evil one. They are not of the world, just as I am not of the world. Sanctify them in the truth; your word is truth. As you sent me into the world, so I have sent them into the world." Clearly, we can see that Jesus is not of the world, his followers are not of this world, *and* we are not to be of this world. The emphasis here, though, isn't to run from the world but to enter into it more. This is why Jesus said, "As you sent me into the world, so I have sent them into the world." Jesus' mission wasn't to leave the world or distance himself from it, but to come into its fullness yet remain sinless. We are not to become like the world, but we are sent into all the messiness of it. We are called to be experts in knowing how to become immersed in this world but not changed by it. David Mathis suggests we change the phrase "in the world but not of the world" to "not of the world, but sent into the world."[3]

Luke made it clear that the early church was not some holy huddle. They were not living a communal or monastic lifestyle. They were engaged with their culture, and daily people were being added to their number (Acts 2:47). This wasn't simply a reshuffling of Christians; these were new believers. They were filled with the Spirit, and all their knowledge of God, their worship, and their intense fellowship thrust them out into the world. The overflow of God's grace and love in their lives made them missional. John Stott said, "The Holy Spirit is a missionary Spirit who created a missionary

---

3. David Mathis, "Let's Revise the Popular Phrase 'In, but Not Of,'" Desiring God, August 29, 2012, https://www.desiringgod.org/articles/lets-revise-the-popular-phrase-in-but-not-of.

church."⁴ The missional activity in this church wasn't programed or forced; it was a natural expression of what they were experiencing.

Being missional means caring about what God cares about: lost, broken people. A missional heart desires to be sent into the world. Being missional means knowing and caring about the people you critique. Missional people find themselves eating with tax collectors and sinners. We must eat with the people we want to reach.

Adding Confession to Mission

A confession is a statement that clarifies what we believe. We see confessions all the way back to the time of Moses. "Hear, O Israel: The LORD our God, the LORD is one" (Deut. 6:4). Here Moses was confessing the truth that there is one God, and he is our God. The apostle Peter confessed what he believed to be true about Jesus when he said, "You are the Christ, the Son of the living God" (Matt. 16:16). Paul gave a more comprehensive confession of his belief, saying, "For I delivered to you as of first importance what I also received: that Christ died for our sins in accordance with the Scriptures, that he was buried, that he was raised on the third day in accordance with the Scriptures" (1 Cor. 15:3–4). There is a confession in Paul's letter to the church in Ephesus that most scholars think was already in existence and being used during baptisms before Paul ever wrote it. Paul called this a trustworthy saying: "There is one body and one Spirit—just as you were called to the one hope that belongs to your call—one Lord, one faith, one baptism, one God and Father of all, who is over all and through all and in all" (Eph. 4:4–6).

The church fathers in the second and third centuries also developed confessions. We know them now as creeds. *Creed* simply means

---

4. John Stott, *The Spirit, the Church, and the World: The Message of Acts* (Downers Grove, IL: InterVarsity, 1990), 86.

"believe." Creeds clarify what early Christians believed the Bible to be saying. Each of these creeds came about because false teaching was coming into the churches, and the church leaders wanted to clarify their beliefs in a way that would clearly show the differences between Christian doctrine and false teaching. The Nicene Creed came about to fight the Arians, who did not believe Jesus was God. The Apostles' Creed came about to fight Gnosticism creeping into the church. Much later, during the Protestant Reformation in the sixteenth and seventeenth centuries, new and more extensive confessions were developed to give as much clarity as possible to differentiate their belief from those of the Roman Catholic Church. These confessions include the Westminster Confession, the Heidelberg Confession, and the London Baptist Confession. These were major historic moments of clarity about what a church believes, which is why we don't have a new confession for every new generation.

Some have pushed back on the whole idea of a confession with statements like "No creed but Christ" or "No creed but the Bible." But this is problematic in a few ways, not least of which is the fact that they themselves are creeds. This opposition to confessions misunderstands them as attempts to in some way usurp the Bible and instead follow manmade documents. The whole point of creeds or confessions isn't to usurp Scripture, but to bring clarity to it.

When the teaching of the Bible is clear, good doctrine is protected. This helps us contend for the faith. It helps us become rocks that the waves of the ocean break against instead of driftwood tossed to and fro (Eph. 4:14). It also allows churches from different traditions to be united on the things that matter most and gives us freedom to disagree on secondary and tertiary issues. Clarity through confessions frees us from the blinders of our current age. By subscribing to confessions, we are not relying on our own interpretation or the prevailing view of the church in a particular generation. We are, instead, standing on the good deposit given to us from the church across all ages.

Being a confessional church is crucial to being clear about what we believe the Bible to be saying and to build on a sure theological foundation. Without the confession, we are like the Leaning Tower of Pisa. I (Jim) lived within walking distance of that tower for four years. I would take our dog to play on the grass around the tower and look at the massive bell tower where the top leans some twenty feet south of the bottom. The tower leans because it was built on a poor foundation. The ground there isn't rock; it's soft sand that can't support the structure. The church, though, was built on the good foundation of Peter and his confession that Jesus is "the Christ, the son of the living God" (Matt. 16:16).

Churches looking to add confession to their missional DNA should first consider clarifying what it is they confess. Then they should ask how they plan to teach *all* of what they believe to large, medium, and small groups, and how they will call their people to what God defines as flourishing.

Confession and Mission Combined

At the intersection of confession and mission, love flourishes. This is why Paul said, "If I speak in the tongues of men and of angels, but have not love, I am a noisy gong or clanging cymbal. And if I have prophetic powers, and understand all mysteries and all knowledge, and if I have all faith, so as to remove mountains, but have not love, I am nothing. If I give away all I have, and if I deliver up my body to be burned, but have not love, I gain nothing" (1 Cor. 13:1–3). Biblical love holds tight to Jesus and all that he teaches but lets loose every other preference that might hinder reaching the world we live in. Biblical love welcomes diversity, discomfort, and awkwardness. Biblical love sacrifices comfort, time, and energy for others to know Jesus. That is the love the Ephesian church had at first, and that is the love that is to mark every church lest we lose our lampstand.

Missional and confessional aren't two opposing ideas we need to hold in tension; they are two truths designed to work together. Nobody has illustrated how these two truths complement each other better than Jesus. His lifetime of sinlessness means he never failed at either. He never had to choose between them. In him we have a perfect model. He left the comfort of heaven to be sent into the world. He fully entered into the pain of our sinful world to the point of taking on the wrath our sin deserves. No one understands the human experience better than Jesus. No one understands the Word of God better than Jesus. No one is more confessional and missional than Jesus, which makes him uniquely positioned to bring us truth.

Jesus doesn't look down on us; he loves us. He doesn't run from us; he runs toward us. He sees all our thoughts and motivations, and he doesn't abandon us. He doesn't brush over sin; he understands it better than anyone. When Jesus speaks truth, he doesn't use it to look down on us; he uses it to love us. Sometimes that truth is harsh and up-front; sometimes it is subtle and incisive, and sometimes it is delayed until the heart is ready to receive it. In all of these ways, Jesus enters into the mission in order to care and confront. There is no confession or mission without Jesus. He is the One we confess and the King who gave us the mission. He is the reason truth and love are not in contradiction. Truth declares we deserve condemnation. Rather than compromising truth and pretending that wasn't the case, or leaving us to wallow in our sin, Jesus perfectly upheld truth while perfectly loving the world on the cross.

Timothy George encapsulated this well in an address he gave on the day he founded Beeson Divinity School:

> In the lingo of contemporary labels, we will be neither a haven for disaffected liberalism nor a bastion of raucous fundamentalism. We will be evangelical but also ecumenical, conservative but not irresponsible, confessional yet interdenominational. Above all, I pray that we might be a school where heart and head go hand in

hand, where the love of God and pursuit of truth join forces in the formation of men and women, called by God, empowered by His Holy Spirit, equipped for the ministry of His church, sent forth into the world to bear witness to the grace of God revealed in the person of Jesus Christ, whom to know is life eternal.[5]

Churches that embody confession and mission produce fruitful disciples who know how to live in this world and engage this world without becoming like this world. As Christians we are living in a form of exile away from the home we are created for, and we must equip our people to thrive as exiles in the world we live in. That is the focus of the next chapter.

---

5. Timothy George, "Installation of Timothy George as Founding Dean," Beeson Divinity School, February 21, 2019, https://www.beesondivinity.com/blog/2019/timothy -george-installation.

Chapter 14

Embracing Exile

CHOSEN AND EXILED. THAT IS THE NORM FOR GOD'S PEOPLE. IT would be an oxymoron if it weren't God's design. As Peter addressed the early church dispersed about the Roman Empire because of increased persecution in Jerusalem, he opened his letter by saying, "Peter, an apostle of Jesus Christ, to those who are elect exiles of the Dispersion in Pontus, Galatia, Cappadocia, Asia, and Bithynia, according to the foreknowledge of God the Father" (1 Peter 1:1). Christians in the West, especially if we live in the US, and especially if we are white, have enjoyed a seat at the table of power for hundreds of years. But that is changing fast.

Christians today and especially in the coming generations will likely exist on the margins of power. This is not abnormal for God's people, but a return to what has been the norm since the fall in Genesis 3. The most common state for God's people is exile. We don't choose this word lightly. *Exile* means living away from home. Now, we do want to acknowledge that there are blessings that have come with what we call Christendom. We would be naive to think that the opportunity for Christians to vote according to our morals and convictions, to have fair trials, and to worship without threat of prosecution are not real blessings. But we would be equally naive to assume that

Christians in power is always going to go well. History shows us that this is just not the case. The scope of this chapter, however, is to make the case that there are also many blessings in a state of exile and that the church can actually flourish more in that state. Exile comes in two forms. First, there is the kind where God's people are geographically displaced from their home. This is what we saw with Adam and Eve as they were exiled from the garden. This is also what Abraham experienced, for God's promise to him meant moving to a land in which he would be a foreigner and a sojourner the rest of his life. And this is what the Israelites experienced in Egypt, in their wandering toward the promised land, and again later when the Babylonians came in, conquered Judah, and carried off Daniel and many others.

But God's people don't have to experience a geographic move to experience exile. We can remain in the same place yet see that place change around us. I (Jim) have a good friend who is a Mexican American in New Mexico. His family has been there for generations, and he says they didn't cross the border; the border crossed them. They never left New Mexico, but when it ceased to be a province of Mexico and eventually became a part of the United States, the culture changed around them as it became increasingly American and less Mexican. This is similar to what is happening to Christians in the US today. We haven't changed where we live, but where we live is changing fast. And the main question we have to ask is this: Can the church flourish in this new society?

The Bible tells us the answer is absolutely, yes! We need to see the blessings in exile so that we won't be afraid of what is ahead of us; and we need to adequately prepare ourselves and our children to be fruitful in this new reality. I (Jim) used to pastor in Oxford, Mississippi, the buckle of the Bible Belt, where I enjoyed social benefits of being a pastor like free golf and discounted luxury items, but when I moved to the largely dechurched context of Orlando, many of those benefits went away. Still, other kingdom blessings quickly presented themselves.

In this chapter, we will look at Acts 11:19–30 to discover six biblical truths about living in exile that we must embrace to navigate our current cultural shift.

Exile Promotes the Advance of the Gospel

In the first three verses of this passage, we see that men and women were scattered all over the empire because of Stephen's execution. These people had lived for generations in Jerusalem and enjoyed a fair measure of autonomy, power, and privilege—until they decided to follow Jesus. They soon lost that power and comfort to the point that many of them had to flee Jerusalem. This is exile.

On the surface, this scattering of God's people might look and feel like bad news. Culture change, especially when it's thrust upon you, can be scary. But the net result of the exile in this passage was kingdom fruit. "There were some of them, men of Cyprus and Cyrene, who on coming to Antioch spoke to the Hellenists also, preaching the Lord Jesus. And the hand of the Lord was with them, and a great number who believed turned to the Lord" (Acts 11:20–21).

It was the believers' very exile that caused the gospel to advance. The gospel will not go forward if people don't go first. We also see that this persecution brought an increased willingness to share their faith. A common thread throughout all of church history is that the more Christians lose in this world for Jesus, the more willing they have been to talk about Jesus. When we enjoy social comforts as Christians, we can be timid in sharing our faith because inherent in that sharing is the risk of losing that comfort if people don't affirm our beliefs. But if we have no comforts, that hindrance to our evangelism is gone. Likewise, the more concerned we are with maintaining power in our culture, the more focused we will be on ourselves instead of others, which can't help but decrease our desire to see others know Jesus.

We also see increased innovation in the way these early Christians shared the gospel. Up until this point, the new Christians in Jerusalem and even many who had been scattered primarily shared the gospel only with the Jews. But in Antioch, somehow, they got the idea to share the gospel with gentiles. This door was opened by Peter in chapter 10 when Cornelius became the first gentile to convert to Christianity. Not only did they see gentile converts, but shockingly, they did not require them to become Jewish first by conforming to the Mosaic law and Jewish customs of the time. This gospel innovation would shape the future of the faith.

This is one parallel between the type of exile we see in Acts and the more extreme exile described in the Old Testament. Exile for both the early church and Israel did not destroy their faith but created a type of necessary creative stimulus for the faith to flourish in a new, albeit challenging, context.

But above all these things, verse 21 makes it clear that there was something supernatural supporting and guiding these events. Luke recorded that "the hand of the Lord was with them." This is a way of saying that God was going before them in every way. They knew that. They saw that. And the gospel went forward more powerfully than it ever had before.

We see here exile serving to promote the advance of the gospel. And if this is generally true, and we believe it is, then we can logically say that not living in exile over the past few hundred years, having comfort and power in society as Christians, has hindered gospel progress. Christians in comfort and power do not tend to rely on God for basic things when we think we can control them. Christians living in a society that generally affirms our beliefs on paper are pushed to choose between that faith and inevitable cultural gaps between what is on paper and what actually happens in that culture. We Christians who do not publicly suffer for our faith are less able to encourage or challenge the faith of others watching.

We aren't saying we should desire or seek persecution or exile, but we will need to embrace it when it comes. Churches may have been full in the twentieth century, but that doesn't mean they were full of Christians. Now that the tide is turning and we are in the largest and fastest religious shift in the history of our country, the need to prepare for and embrace exile will serve to advance the gospel in our generation.

Exile Confronts Our Idols of Power

Acts 11:22 says that the report of what was happening came to the church in Jerusalem, and they sent Barnabas to investigate. We can imagine how uncomfortable and maybe even threatened the church in Jerusalem might have felt as power and influence in the global church shifted from Jerusalem to Antioch, which would become the most influential church in the world for a time. The center of Christianity was moving.

Every bit of power the men in Jerusalem had enjoyed was confronted here. Not only were they losing power in their old culture because of their faith in Jesus, but now they were losing influence in their new Christian culture. We don't know how these early Christians in Jerusalem dealt with this kind of power and influence being taken from them, but they certainly had to deal with it. We know Barnabas was chosen to go and check it out. He was the perfect person to send. He was humble, and he was more concerned with the kingdom of God than with any power he might have in this world. He wasn't concerned with these gentiles having to conform to his culture; he was concerned with these gentiles conforming to Christ.

About three years ago, I (Jim) made a statement in a sermon that I didn't expect to be controversial, but it turned out to be. I said, "If I have the privilege of pastoring Orlando Grace Church for the next two decades, a real part of my ministry will be walking with predominantly white Christians through the loss of power in our society."

People asked me, "Why would you say such a thing? Christians in power protect our society." I understood what they were asking. Jesus does say we are the salt of the earth, which has a preserving quality to the surrounding culture. But this has happened most effectively over church history from a bottom up posture of humility, not power. The early church operated from the margins of societal influence, but in just a few generations, Christianity had spread throughout the Roman Empire and was challenging much of that culture's ethical foundations. In addition, we would be naive to say that "Christians" in power has always worked out well for society or the Christian witness as it was professing Christians in power in the West who propagated injustices to Native Americans, slavery, and segregation.

We are to seek the good of our cities, and this can be done without being at the table of influence. God told the Israelite exiles through Jeremiah that they were to seek the good of their new cities from the margins of power. "Thus says the Lord of hosts, the God of Israel, to all the exiles whom I have sent into exile from Jerusalem to Babylon: . . . seek the welfare of the city where I have sent you into exile, and pray to the Lord on its behalf, for in its welfare you will find your welfare" (Jer. 29:4–7).

The margins of power may not be attractive or comfortable, but we take heart in the fact that God used Christians mightily in the early church in that context, and he is still doing that today in the global East and South. We can be the city on the hill without being on Capitol Hill. We can be salt without being in power. Whatever happens to the culture in the United States, the kingdom of God will be fine.

Exile Is Where We Depend on the Lord

When Barnabas arrived at Antioch, he saw the grace of God on these people. He wasn't jealous; he was glad. Barnabas was full of the Holy

Spirit and gave them one exhortation: Remain faithful to the Lord with steadfast purpose. That was their only hope in exile!

My (Jim's) kids are at an age where they aren't always convinced I know what I'm talking about. They don't always like to hear the instructions I give. They can sometimes act like they'd be just fine out on their own—until a loud thunderstorm comes or a movie gets scary or (God forbid) the power goes out at night or they get lost at Disney. Then the thing they want most in the world is their parents. Sometimes we have to be in a difficult situation to be reminded where our hope comes from. Difficulty can quickly reorient our priorities.

And I won't mince words here: Exile does bring difficulty. We don't want to be naive about that. It has and is currently costing Christians in the East, Middle East, and North Africa their freedoms and sometimes even their lives. But exile reminds us where our true hope is. Joni Eareckson Tada has been in a wheelchair for more than fifty years as a result of a diving accident when she was young. Something she said has always stuck with me in the most uncomfortable way.

> I sure hope I can bring this wheelchair to heaven. Now, I know that's not theologically correct. But I hope to bring it and put it in a little corner of heaven, and then in my new, perfect, glorified body, standing on grateful glorified legs, I'll stand next to my Savior, holding his nail-pierced hands. I'll say, "Thank you, Jesus," and he will know that I mean it, because he knows me. He'll recognize me from the fellowship we're now sharing in his sufferings. And I will say, "Jesus, do you see that wheelchair? You were right when you said that in this world we would have trouble, because that thing was a lot of trouble. But the weaker I was in that thing, the harder I leaned on you. And the harder I leaned on you, the stronger I discovered you to be. It never would have happened had you not given me the bruising of the blessing of that wheelchair."[1]

---

1. Joni Eareckson Tada, *Hope . . . The Best of Things* (Wheaton, IL: Crossway, 2008), 29.

Now, Joni's suffering was not a result of exile, but it still makes the point well. Wheelchairs or not, we are spiritual people exiled into broken bodies because of our sin. But we will be brought back from this exile into renewed bodies because our exile is temporary. When we are most aware that the world we live in is not our home, we are the most dependent on him who has made a home for us and is bringing us there.

Exile Shows Us Our New and Better Identity

As we continue reading Acts 11, we get to this fascinating verse: "And in Antioch the disciples were first called Christians" (v. 26). This name was given to them by non-Christians. The early Christians had names for themselves like "the Way" or "the disciples," but to everyone else they were an enigma. Up to this point, there had been a great cultural divide between Jews and Gentiles in the Roman Empire. Now there was this new group of people composed of both. Nothing in that day brought these two groups of people together. It was such a radically countercultural thing that the people in Antioch gave them a new name: Christians. Christ-ones. They were no longer defined by their ethnicities; they were defined by their association with Jesus.

God's people have always been identified with God over context. God gave Israel their identity in the wilderness at Mount Sinai when he made a covenant with them, not once they went into the promised land. This means that their identity was not conditional upon entering the land. They couldn't lose it when they were exiled, and neither can we. God didn't make us his people when we were at the height of social power. It wasn't after the church became socially acceptable that he made us his. Therefore, we will not be any less his if the church loses social standing we were never promised. The early church's identity was not in Rome. It was not in their strength, power, or security for they had none. Their identity was in Jesus—so much so that people who weren't even Christians gave them the name Christ-ones.

The years 2020 and 2021 brought many tensions into our society and into our churches, including racial tensions. In that season, someone told me (Jim) that there are other churches for "those" types of people, meaning people who were not white or culturally like him. That is one of the most unchristian things a person could possibly say. It undermines our new identity as Christ-ones. When we trust in Christ, God no longer sees our sin; he sees the righteousness of Jesus Christ. God doesn't love some future version of us; he loves us—not because we earned it, but because Jesus earned it for us. We now have an allegiance that becomes our identity, and it is greater than any other identity we have, including ethnicity.

Exile, however, has a way of stripping us of anything else that we might cling to as our chief identity. When social status is stripped away; when national identity is stripped away; when money, freedoms, and security are stripped from us, our true identity in Christ becomes clearer and sweeter. But there are some important precautions we must take if our identity in Christ is going to sustain us in exile, which leads us to the fifth thing we see in this passage about exile.

Exile Requires Discipleship

In Acts 11:25 we find that Barnabas went to Tarsus to look for Saul, then brought him back to Antioch, and together they taught the church for a whole year. I love that Barnabas could see that, at some level, he was out of his depth here and went to look for the apostle Paul. Barnabas's value for discipleship was so great that he went all the way to Tarsus to get the best teacher he could find for this new church.

Discipleship requires humility as we build the kingdom by building people. It forces us to listen to and learn from voices we might not otherwise have heard. White Christians are experiencing a sense of exile maybe for the first time in the US, but Christians in other demographics have always felt like exiles. If we are seeking the best teachers for our current moment, we would be wise to listen to people who have ministered from a place of exile in the US for generations.

Considering the world our children and grandchildren will likely grow up in, the need for discipleship is great. New Christians don't have the Biblical foundation our culture used to provide. We must make it our aim as church leaders to teach the Bible in our sermons. We must invest in Christian adult education. The main goal of our youth ministry, as much fun as it may be, has to be discipleship. If we rely solely on entertaining worship or memorable experiences, we will fall short of our goal, and our children will bear the cost of our shortsightedness. The more we enter exile, the greater the need in the church for true discipleship.

Exile Makes Us Generous

If you need evidence that God explicitly wants his people's reaction to exile to be generosity in the places we are sent, look no further than the passage from Jeremiah referenced earlier. God told his people to pray for and seek the good of the communities they were sent to because their own personal good was tied to the good of the people they lived with.

But Acts 11 fleshes this out even more. Some prophets came from Jerusalem to Antioch, and one named Agabus, filled with the Spirit, foretold a great famine that, in fact, came to be. It's well recorded during the reign of Claudius that a flood in the Nile destroyed the whole Egyptian harvest, and the price of grain skyrocketed in the Middle East. So, every Christian, according to their ability, gave relief to the Christians who needed it most in that region.

Exile brought out generous hearts in these believers because they couldn't live in exile and be entitled or stingy at the same time. This kind of unusual generosity didn't just help out other believers; they in turn were generous to others in their communities, even unbelievers. Unbelievers can see from our generosity that we have radically different value systems. They can see that we are not living for ourselves but for Jesus, and this makes an impact. And, as we said in the beginning of this chapter, this exile set the stage for such an explosion of the gospel that in just four centuries even the Roman emperor would claim Christ as Lord.

Back to the initial question: Can the church flourish in our changing culture? Yes. God purposely uses exile for his people to sanctify us and to strengthen and grow his kingdom. Isaiah 24 prophesies the shaking of Jerusalem. God shook his people's earthly city to pieces so they might see their unshakable citizenship in heaven.

And we can trust in God's goodness in exile because no one has ever known exile like Jesus Christ. He who was in the very form of God emptied himself to take on the form of a servant. He willingly took on exile from the heavenly throne room where glory, comfort, and joy knew no limits, to enter this world of pain, sorrow, and shame. His exile culminated on the cross as he, in the words of the author of Hebrews, "suffered outside the gate in order to sanctify the people through his own blood" (Heb. 13:12).

Jesus' exile means that while we may experience exile from the world we live in, we will never experience exile from the God who loves us. He will be with us always, and he will take us to a home one day from which no one will ever be exiled. The gospel is both the reason for our temporary exile now and the hope of our eternal security in our heavenly home with our Savior.

Chapter 15

Five Exhortations to Church Leaders

THE SHEER NUMBER OF PEOPLE DEPARTING THE CHURCH RIGHT now can be hard to digest, leaving us to wonder if they can be brought back. We have to be careful not to write them off, but also not to write off the clear instruction we are given in the Bible either. Beginning in the 1700s, the Enlightenment leaders saw the rise of scientific study as a threat to what the Bible teaches because of the inability to scientifically prove the miracles we read about in the Bible. Critical scholars at the time then decided to remove from the Bible whatever did not align with our scientific advancements in the hopes of saving Christianity. But what remained was not Christianity. Removing the supernatural elements in the name of "saving Christianity" did more harm than good.

This isn't a mistake we want to repeat. We must hold up a mirror to the church and honestly analyze what contributions we are making to the Great Dechurching, but we can't allow the pendulum to swing too far to the other side and do whatever we can to accommodate our surrounding culture only to bring people into a community that we simply cannot call the church. In this final chapter, we take an introspective look by hearing five exhortations from the Bible that we must heed if we are to thread this needle effectively. Three of these exhortations came from Jesus, one from Peter, and one from Paul.

Exhortation 1: Don't Be Surprised When People Fall Away

The reality is that some dechurched people can be won back, but others were never a part of the true church to begin with. Jesus warned his disciples, and us, of this fact in Matthew 13, where he was confusing an impromptu crowd by the sea by speaking in parables to them as a form of judgment on their unbelief. But, to his disciples, he explained the parables. They were warnings about misconceptions of the kingdom Jesus was bringing. He didn't want them to be surprised when the kingdom didn't come in exactly the way they expected it to.

> He put another parable before them, saying, "The kingdom of heaven may be compared to a man who sowed good seed in his field, but while his men were sleeping, his enemy came and sowed weeds among the wheat and went away. So when the plants came up and bore grain, then the weeds appeared also. And the servants of the master of the house came and said to him, 'Master, did you not sow good seed in your field? How then does it have weeds?' He said to them, 'An enemy has done this.' So the servants said to him, 'Then do you want us to go and gather them?' But he said, 'No, lest in gathering the weeds you root up the wheat along with them. Let both grow together until the harvest, and at harvest time I will tell the reapers, "Gather the weeds first and bind them in bundles to be burned, but gather the wheat into my barn."'"
> (Matt. 13:24–30)

While we have explored ways to better understand and reach those who are dechurching, we also have to acknowledge the reality that some portion of this group were not Christians in the first place. In their case, what has always been true is now revealed. As the social pressures to identify as Christian in our culture are removed and as new pressures mount to discourage people from identifying as Christian, many who were never Christians in the first place are finally able to freely walk away. We should not be surprised when people fall away from the visible church. The invisible church is the true number of all believers in the world, and the visible church is merely what we can see. There is a lot of overlap, but some people in the visible church are not believers. These are the weeds growing alongside the wheat.

This falling away happens in different ways. Some just show their true colors when church becomes socially or politically inconvenient. This is the young man who chooses to leave the church for a beautiful young girl who wants nothing to do with the church. These are at least some of the people who decided during the COVID-19 lockdowns to take up new Sunday morning activities and leave worship behind. These are people on both the secular left and the secular right who left because the church wasn't feeding their political idols.

When my (Jim's) kids were young, a Sunday school teacher in our church who was also in our community group abruptly decided he was no longer a Christian and that he was leaving the church and his family. As you can imagine, this stunned a lot of people in our church. Consider also the public departures of people like former pastor Josh Harris or the public falls of people like apologist Ravi Zacharias. These things have caused large numbers of people to be thrown into confusion, and some of them will decide to leave the church as well.

The natural question we might ask is, what in the world just happened? Notice that this is precisely the question the servants asked. They went to the master and asked if the seed was bad from the beginning. They expected the seed to be pure, but it was not. We expect the church to be pure, but it won't be until Jesus comes back.

Paul told the Corinthian church, "Even Satan disguises himself as an angel of light. So it is no surprise if his servants, also, disguise themselves as servants of righteousness. Their end will correspond to their deeds" (2 Cor. 11:14–15). The apostle John wrote, "They went out from us, but they were not of us; for if they had been of us, they would have continued with us. But they went out, that it might become plain that they all are not of us" (1 John 2:19).

In every age and in every place, people will leave the church. Jesus told us this, so we must not be surprised or overreact when it happens.

Exhortation 2:
Extreme Responses Hurt People

Extreme responses hurt people, and we need to be careful not to swing to one of two extremes. We can't throw up our hands and stop striving for the purity of the church on one extreme, but we also can't become overly strict and rigid, expecting that we will make the church perfectly pure on the other. My (Jim's) wife, Angela, was telling me recently about a study of sex addicts in which 77 percent of the sex addicts surveyed reported growing up in an overly controlling household.[1] Eighty-seven percent of sex addicts surveyed reported growing up in disengaged families. Households that drift to the extreme of lack of control and households that drift to the extreme of overcontrol both harm their children. The same is true in the church.

The first extreme is to say, "Well, Jesus said it would be a mixed

---

1. Brought to my attention by Tim Burkholder in a lecture on human sexuality at Reformed Theological Seminary, Orlando, Florida. Originally from Patrick Carnes, *Don't Call it Love: Recovery from Sexual Addiction* (New York: Bantam, 1992), table 5-1, p. 146.

bag, so why try to push people toward a Christian ethic or a local church, or why care if they believe things like the resurrection?" That would be harmful because we would be shortchanging the people we are ministering to by dismantling the richness of the belief, belonging, and behavior that Jesus calls us into.

The church that emphasizes the number of people in attendance at the expense of discipleship is, in a sense, throwing up their hands in the areas of behavior and belonging to focus on belief. The church that creates community around freethinking is throwing their hands up in the areas of belief and behavior to focus on belonging. Jesus tells us that after we address the log in our own eye, we *should* help someone else with the splinter in their eye. This is why we have church membership, it's why we have discipleship, and in extreme cases, this is why we have church discipline as it is laid out in the Bible.

On the other hand, we can't operate under an attitude of suspicion, looking at every person and wondering, *Are you a weed? Are you a son of Satan?* That hyperfocus on behavior comes at the expense of belief and belonging. It's the equivalent of going in after the weeds early on and trampling the good shoots of wheat under your foot or accidentally pulling up the good shoots with the bad ones.

My (Jim's) kids are currently under the impression that everyone who drives a white van is a criminal. No exceptions. I'm sorry if you drive a big white van because my kids will look at you as if you are a kidnapper or maybe even a murderer. We were driving to school one morning, and we saw a big white van for a business that helps people with special needs get from one part of town to the next. It's a really great service. But my daughter looked at that van and said, "See, Daddy, it literally says on that van, 'We Will Take You!'" That's basically what the church does to its people when they drift to this other extreme by trying to pull up all the weeds, regardless of who else gets pulled up in the process. We are called to believe the best until the situation is clear. An attitude of suspicion is condescending, harmful to others, and isolating to those who embrace it.

So, how will you know it when you see it? Often people will turn a nonmoral issue into a moral issue because behind it is the suspicion that you are not really following Jesus. One time a man pulled me (Jim) aside after my wife, Angela, decided to go back to school to pursue a Master's degree in counseling. He said, "I'm really proud of Angela for wanting to grow, but I don't think a woman's place is in the workforce." What he meant was, "I'm suspicious that women who work are inevitably going to neglect their families, so I'm going to make working a moral issue, and if you don't conform, I question your walk with Jesus." And then he applied that preexisting misconception to Angela. That's not pushing people toward Christ; that is an overly controlling posture with a hyperfocus on behavior that causes people harm.

Many of the people dechurching today are casualties of the church moving to one of these two extremes. We must hold this balance in tension.

Exhortation 3: Be Patient

Jesus was not telling this story so the disciples could root out all the weeds from the wheat. The servants want to go in right away and take the weeds out. They want to act. But the master says, "No, I have a specialist who can deal with this later." That doesn't make the master uncaring or inactive. The master knows best how to deal with the issue at hand, and so does our heavenly Master.

Jesus said he also has specialists who will deal with this issue at the end of time. Those specialists are called angels. The disciples wanted the fullness of the kingdom to come fast, but Jesus said it would, in fact, be slow. If the disciples were tempted to be impatient, how much more are we? The disciples lived in a slow-moving agrarian society where you had to go out and catch fish or grow wheat to eat. There is nothing immediate about that culture. We get frustrated when both drive-through lanes at Chick-fil-A aren't open. We get irritated when the waiter takes too long with our food. If our computer pauses for ten seconds while loading a website, we want to talk to the internet company. If the disciples in that culture struggled with patience, how much more will we? But the solutions the Bible offers require patience.

Impatience comes in many forms, but here Jesus was warning about being impatient with the slowness of the kingdom. We don't want to wait on God; we want God to conform to our timetable. We want our prayers to be answered immediately. We want pain and fear to stop now. We want our churches to fill back up with some quick, easy fix. We don't need to awkwardly look to the left and right, hyperfocusing on who the weeds are. We need to trust that God knows.

Have you ever seen a live police car chase? From the driver's perspective, he thinks he's getting away with it. Maybe he just sees one police car behind him, so he thinks he can do it, but he doesn't realize there are ten others he can't see and a helicopter above him telling those cars about every turn he makes. Not only that, but the news helicopters are there too, and the whole nation, including us at home, is watching the chase. Then the man wrecks his car and runs behind a fountain to hide. He thinks he has a chance, but we all can see him. He doesn't have a snowball's chance in a hot place of making it out of there! The same is true of weeds and wolves. God sees them even better than that helicopter, and one day angels, instead of police cars, will come. So, we remain patient.

If we truly understood the judgment to come, none of us would want that day hastened for anyone. Judgment is not fun to talk about, but the Bible tells us that when those specialist angels come to usher in God's wrath on humanity, people will wish the mountains would fall on them rather than face that moment. With that in mind, we should be the most patient people in the world with the souls of others.

It's easy to create caricatures of God that oscillate between a vindictive tyrant who is eager to see people burn and a permissive parent who lets the kids do as they please because he just wants the kids to like him. But God is just *and* gracious, patient *and* fair, decisive *and* long-suffering. He is perfect in every way.

And if you need help remembering that, think about how firmly and swiftly God acted at Calvary to show us how much he cares about us and to what extent he will go to save us from our sins. God the Father sent all the wrath we deserve on God the Son that we might come fully into the kingdom.

We don't need to wait until Judgment Day because the weeds and wolves can out themselves. And when they do, the Bible has given us ways to address that when it happens.

But we should be patient for another important reason: weeds can turn into wheat. We became wheat when we surrendered, not as a rebellious driver surrenders to a police officer only to be taken to jail, but as a loved child to a Father God taking us into the kingdom of heaven. For this and all the other reasons, we remain patient.

Exhortation 4: Shepherd the Flock

Peter exhorted elders to "shepherd the flock of God that is among you, exercising oversight, not under compulsion, but willingly, as God would have you; not for shameful gain, but eagerly; not domineering over those in your charge, but being examples to the flock" (1 Peter 5:2–3). Many of the dechurched people we know left the church without any leaders at their church following up with them or even realizing they were gone. The call of those in church leadership is clear: shepherd the flock.

It's hard to imagine that the apostle Paul or any other New Testament authors could have had any category for pastors who do not know their people. We cannot shepherd people we do not know.

We cannot address needs we are not aware of. Some of this shepherding happens in a sermon, but most of it happens through relational discipleship.

My (Jim's) children attend a classical Christian school, and I once asked the head of the school about the most important factor in leading a healthy school. His answer: retention. They focus on those inside the school and the rest works itself out. That principle is also true in the church. God may give certain church leaders a wider platform than their local church, but that does not excuse them from being a real pastor to their people. The needs of a local church do sometimes become greater than one pastor can serve, so the burden then is creating a structure of leaders who can comprehensively care for the flock God has given them.

The concept of shepherding the flock is one of the most neglected in the rise of American evangelicalism. We equate success with size and reach, but that isn't how God describes success in the Bible. So, church leaders, ask yourselves, "Do I know my flock well enough to carry out Peter's exhortation?"

Peter also told us how we should shepherd: not domineering over those in our charge, but being examples to the flock. We know that many of the dechurched have left because of abusive leadership and failing character in their leaders. Church leaders have a greater burden in front of the Lord than the rest of those in the faith. Will we be faithful to that calling? If so, the people will be blessed, and there will await for us the unfading crown of glory.

Exhortation 5: Equip the Saints

If the church were a sports team, it might be appropriate to think of shepherding as the defense and equipping as the offense. The way Paul envisioned the kingdom of God growing is by leaders equipping those in our charge with the tools necessary to go out and reach more people with the gospel of Jesus Christ. This is crystal clear in his letter to the church in Ephesus, where he wrote, "And [Christ] gave the apostles, the prophets, the evangelists, the shepherds and teachers, to equip the saints for the work of ministry, for building up the body of Christ, until we all attain to the unity of the faith and of the knowledge of the Son of God, to mature manhood, to the measure of the stature of the fullness of Christ" (Eph. 4:11–13).

We can improve the way we equip the saints in many ways, but the most important one is prayer. There are forces around us every minute of the day who want our leaders to fall, who want our children to stray, and who want all of us to be more enamored with literally anything other than Jesus. I (Jim) have thought a lot about this in the context of the Lord's Prayer. The disciples came to Jesus and asked, "Lord, teach us [how] to pray" (Luke 11:1). Do you know that in all my years of ministry I don't think I have ever had someone ask me that? I have been asked about parenting. I have been asked where dinosaurs are in the Bible. I have been asked what happens to cats when they die. But I don't think anyone has ever asked me how to pray.

What was so different about the culture of the early believers that they wanted to learn how they should pray? For one thing, they lacked affluence. Why would we today pray for our daily bread when we can buy whatever we want at the grocery store or go and get it already prepared at Chick-fil-A? When would we have time to think about prayer when we have things to entertain us at every moment? We might think about praying, but then the phone pings and tells us that there is a new dance trend on Instagram. Surely God understands that! John Piper once said, "One of the great uses of Twitter and Facebook will be to prove at the Last Day that prayerlessness was not from lack of time."[2]

---

2. John Piper, "One of the great uses of Twitter and Facebook will be to prove at the Last Day that prayerlessness was not from lack of time," Twitter, October 20, 2009, 5:02 p.m., https://twitter.com/johnpiper/status/5027319857?lang=en.

In his book *A Praying Life*, Paul Miller wrote, "If you are not praying it may well be because you are quietly confident that time, money, and talent are all you need in life to overcome."[3] Miller came to my (Jim's) former church and led a conference on prayer, and the first thing he did was ask us to pray silently. It felt like forever. People were literally looking out of the corners of their eyes to see if they were the only ones who had run out of things to pray for. Do you know how long he gave us to pray? Four minutes! And that was too long for most of the church. That says about all we need to know about our culture.

The way your context will be reached is not primarily through sermons or great worship music. The way a city is reached is through the people in our congregations being built up and sent out. A football coach knows that success on the field depends on the equipping of the players, and a similar principle is at play in the church. The way forward is not by creating something completely new but by returning to something very old.

The Church at a Crossroads

The American church today is at a crossroads. While the kingdom of God will go on, its future in this country is not certain. The first path at this crossroads is the path of fighting for power and influence in society. If we choose this path, we put our supreme hopes in political parties and talk news personalities. We show our disdain for the culture we live in on social media. We make the walls between the world and the church as high as possible, shielding us from the world's influence. We compromise our doctrines and do gymnastics with the Bible to maintain some semblance of a following. We live

---

3. Paul Miller, *A Praying Life: Connecting with God in a Distracting World* (Colorado Springs: NavPress, 2009), 47.

in the past. We live in denial. This path will diminish our gospel witness, and it will relegate the church to inevitable irrelevance for generations.

The second path is to embrace our position as exiles, exercising our influence from the margins of power instead of its seat. It will require a hard look at our churches and church leaders to make sure we are embodying a Christlike vision of mission built out of confession. It will mean taking a hard look at how we interact with the world around us and those under the same roof. It will require continual filling with the Holy Spirit and constant prayer. It will require humble hearts. But this is the path that will lead to the flourishing of the church, its members being built up, and Jesus being glorified in our country and time.

We believe there is hope. Opportunities abound in parenting, college ministry, racial equity, community mental health, healthy institutions, sound doctrine, and simply displaying the fruit of the Spirit in our lives. The path forward is not easy, but it is simple. The marriage of Christianity with American values has provided some good things that we want to be thankful for. We have had religious freedom, money, and technology to export the gospel to the world, biblical teaching at our fingertips, and seminaries to train future leaders. We would be naive and ungrateful not to acknowledge these blessings.

But this marriage has hindered us in other ways. It has created idols of freedom not promised to us in the Bible. It has produced celebrity pastors whose megachurches outgrow their character. It has produced unholy bedfellows with political parties requiring the church to compromise on basic Christian ethical issues and allowing the polarization of our national politics to fracture our churches. We believe God is calling us to more.

The weight of the reality of those departing the church in America can cause us to want to put our heads in the sand. We must not simply watch those leaving and say, "They were the wrong sort of people," or "They left because they were in the wrong sort of church," as we continue business as usual. Instead, we need to allow that weight to sit as long as required to create positive restorative action.

Thankfully, we are offered comfort in Scripture. When the Jews were expelled from Jerusalem after its destruction in 587 BC, God gave the prophet Ezekiel a vision. The vision, which has often puzzled interpreters, was of the throne of heaven sitting on wheels, going out from the temple to the east gate, in the direction of Babylon. This has often been seen as a horrific vision, since it depicts the glory of God leaving the temple. In one sense, it is horrific because it highlights the absolute destruction that had come upon the city of God's people. But in another sense, it is a great comfort to know that God sits on a throne with "wheels" because it means he wasn't stuck there when the people were carried away from the city. Rather, when God allowed his people to be taken away into captivity in the East, he picked up his throne and all his glory and went with them.

In the New Testament, specifically in Matthew 28:19–20, we find the same reality of God's pursuing presence. But this time God's people were in a radically different context. In this case, God didn't send an inaccessibly transcendent vision; he made a clear and simple promise. Here God's people were not being taken; they were being sent. It was not a punishment; it was a commissioning. The fullness of God's glory would go with them (Col. 1:19), all wrapped up in a sympathetic (Heb. 4:15) and gentle (Matt. 11:29) body. And this time it would depart permanently from a city that could be shaken, headed in the direction of a kingdom that couldn't be shaken (Heb. 12:27–28). The people of God were, in one sense, exiles again (1 Peter 1:1). As exiles today, we are not looking forward to rebuilding a city with less glory than the one we left (Ezra 3:12). We look toward the glory of the new Zion, the greater and more beautiful city, which is lit by the glory of Jesus' face (Rev. 21:23).

Having this heavenly city and this compassionate Savior and his Spirit as our Great Comforter, we have no need to trivialize what is lost when people leave the church in droves. We don't have to pretend they weren't true friends or that it didn't hurt or that we were perfect and it was all their fault. This greater comfort allows us to acknowledge and sit with the gravity of grief that rightfully accompanies the Great Dechurching, since we have this hope as an anchor for our souls. It allows us to own our responsibility for the departing, whatever that may be, knowing that our shame and our punishment have been borne by another. Despite even our worst failings, the church will be presented as a spotless bride when the King returns for her (Eph. 5:27). That's not because her (and our) sins weren't real; it's because they were really paid for (Isa. 1:18).

Moreover, having the comfort of Christ and his gospel means we have something to offer those who may one day, by God's grace, choose to return. Because if they do, and some of them will, it will be incumbent upon us not to stay back and glare in suspicion and jealousy like the older brother. If we are still here when that moment comes, it will be our responsibility to drop everything and run alongside the Father to welcome them home. To remain in the church means to continue to identify as a child of the Father, and ours is a Father who runs after prodigals. Let us then pray for grace to remain and grace to run.

The Great Dechurching could well be the American church's most crucial moment and greatest opportunity. As church leaders, we consider it the privilege of a lifetime to serve in this moment.

But while he was still a long way off, his father saw him and felt compassion, and ran and embraced him.
—LUKE 15:20

Acknowledgments

I (JIM) THANK MY WIFE, ANGELA, FOR HER SUPPORT AND GUIDANCE in this research and writing. As a student at Reformed Theological Seminary, Orlando, and an aspiring mental health professional, her vantage point on this topic has been invaluable. Thanks also to my four children, Turner, Collins, Ivey, and James, for enduring the writing grind, and to my parents, Bob and Katherine Davis, for helping out with those children along the way.

I (Michael) thank my wife, Sara, and kids, Joey and London, for their insight and patience during late nights and long hours of research and writing.

We thank Collin Hansen and Justin Holcomb for encouraging us to turn the research into a book and for their assistance navigating the complexities of publishing.

We thank Dr. Ryan Burge for his excellence in data analytics, interpretation, research best practices, and insights in the book itself.

We thank Dr. Paul Djupe for his work on study design, attention to compliance, and use of common language between other historic surveys and studies.

We thank Kyle Rohane, Alexis De Weese, and the Zondervan Reflective team for their belief in the project and excellence in editing, marketing, and publicity.

We especially thank Renee Jackson for crafting fictional narrative around the dechurching profiles and tying those insights cohesively into the text.

We thank Jonathan Prudhomme, Robert Jackson, and Skyler Flowers for their ideas, writing contributions, and feedback.

We thank Kelly Simpson, John Ellis, Michael Aitcheson, and Brenda-Lee Miller for their helpful feedback on the manuscript.

We thank Tim Keller and John Frame for their lives, thoughts, examples, and contribution to the church.